BUILDING
YOUR
PORTFOLIO

The CILIP guide

Every purchase of a Facet book helps to fund CILIP's advocacy, awareness and accreditation programmes for information professionals.

BUILDING YOUR PORTFOLIO

The CILIP guide

THIRD EDITION

Kath Owen
Margaret Watson

facet publishing

© Margaret Watson 2008, 2010
© Margaret Watson and Kath Owen 2015

Published by Facet Publishing
7 Ridgmount Street, London WC1E 7AE
www.facetpublishing.co.uk

Facet Publishing is wholly owned by CILIP: the Chartered
Institute of Library and Information Professionals.

British Library Cataloguing in Publication Data
A catalogue record for this book is available from the British
Library.

ISBN 978-1-78330-020-4

First published 2008
Second edition 2010
This third edition 2015

Text printed on FSC accredited material.

Typeset from authors' files in 11/15 pt Aldine 721 and Chantilly by
Facet Publishing Production.
Printed and made in Great Britain by CPI Group (UK) Ltd,
Croydon, CR0 4YY.

Contents

Contributors

Sarah Cockroft

Sarah works for Calderdale Libraries. She started as a library assistant, became a supervisor within Calderdale Libraries; later, after gaining skills and qualifications, she was promoted to be the team leader for nine libraries, an art gallery and three mobile libraries. She gained her ACLIP qualification in 2009.

Linda Coombs

Linda (@LVCoombs, lvcoombs@gmail.com) is Librarian at Tresham College, Northamptonshire. She was one of the first candidates to use the regulations introduced in 2014.

Roberta Crossley

Roberta has worked for Calderdale Libraries since 1978. In 1987 she gained the City & Guilds Library and Information Assistants Certificate at Huddersfield Technical College, being tutored by Margaret Chapman. She was pleasantly surprised to bump into Margaret some 22 years later in 2009 when undertaking her ACLIP. She is team leader for Calderdale Libraries West Area.

Nicola Forgham-Healey

Nicola manages an NHS medical library. She has been a librarian for 11 years and has held a range of library and information roles in the NHS and academic sectors. She has been actively involved in the profession, and held a number of committee posts at divisional and national level. She has helped to organize and run a number of national conferences for the Career Development Group and has published a number of articles on continuing professional development (CPD). She is a CILIP mentor and has a professional interest in online learning.

Chloe French

After completing an undergraduate degree in English and German studies at the University of Birmingham, Chloe spent a year as a graduate trainee at the Institute of Advanced Legal Studies library. She studied for an MA in library and information studies at University College London and joined West Sussex Library Service as a trainee librarian. She currently works as a librarian at Crawley Library.

Donna Gundry

Donna is Head of Library Services at Plymouth College of Art, a newly created higher education (HE) institution. She is a member of the publication committee group and lead researcher for the Art Libraries Society (ARLIS). Having worked in public and academic libraries for eight years, she was awarded her MCLIP in 2013, and is now a mentor. She studied her postgraduate degree in library and information studies at Robert Gordon University, graduating in 2011.

Jim Jackson

A keen advocate for frontline staff and the continued development of the Framework of Qualifications, Jim is the Career Development Champion for Library and Culture Services at the University of Exeter. He has been involved in various types of staff development training for over 15 years and has taken part in a wide range of activities. Jim worked with CILIP in the development of the Framework of Qualifications and was the first person in the country to be awarded Certification status with CILIP. He has spoken at many events organized by CILIP and to a wide range of external organizations about staff training and development.

His role as Career Development Champion is to offer support and guidance to those seeking to further their careers, locally and nationally.

Heather Karpicki

Heather has worked as a library assistant in public libraries, at the area's headquarters, as a travelling library supervisor, and as a bibliotherapist before moving into her current role as team leader for Central Area, Calderdale Libraries. She enjoys engaging with the community and promoting local studies. She gained her ACLIP qualification in 2009.

Ayub Khan

Ayub is Customer Services Manager (face to face) at Warwickshire County Council. He is a former board member of CILIP's Chartership Board. He has held a number of posts in public libraries specializing in school librarianship, young people's librarianship and community librarianship. He has served as a CILIP councillor and is a former Career Development Group president. He was awarded an MBE for services to libraries in 2013.

Pam Martindale

Pam is a member of the CILIP Professional Registration and Accreditation Board. Formerly a strategic manager for Cornwall Library Service, she is now retired and is an enthusiastic advocate of Twitter. Pam is active in the South West Regional Member Network as a mentor and contributes to professional registration workshops.

Karen Newton

Karen has had a long and varied career with Sunderland Public Libraries. She is currently Hub Services Manager. After working on the pilot project for the ACLIP, Karen enrolled on the part-time BSc (Hons) information studies course at Northumbria University, which she completed in 2010. Karen freely admits that she would never have thought of undertaking such a course if CILIP's Certification Scheme had not helped her to realize her capabilities. She is currently Web Editor for the Branch and Mobile Libraries Group.

Kath Owen

Kath chairs the CILIP Professional Registration and Accreditation Board and was a member of the Future Skills Project Board, which worked on professional registration and the PKSB. Until her retirement, Kath was a senior manager in Nottinghamshire Public Libraries with a particular interest in staff development. She revalidated her Fellowship in 2014.

Lesley Randall

Lesley is a Senior Librarian working for Wandsworth Borough Council. She has a particular interest in reader development. She started her work towards Certification when it was first introduced and then moved on to achieve Chartership in 2009.

Shamin Renwick

Shamin is an academic librarian at The University of the West Indies, St Augustine, Trinidad and Tobago, and has presented conference papers, workshops and posters. Shamin has written several refereed publications and has co-edited the books *Caribbean Libraries in the 21st Century* (2007) and *Directory of Caribbean Agricultural Information Sources* (2009). She is the recipient of several awards, including the Chartered Fellowship of CILIP (FCLIP).

Pooja Tejura

Pooja is a library assistant at Sutton Library Service with wide experience in customer care, library catalogue information systems, and day-to-day library management. She has contributed to raising the profile of Sutton Library Service by understanding that each library branch has a unique customer base and role within the community, requiring her to tailor events, develop new skills and enhance her knowledge accordingly. Pooja was one of the first candidates to complete Certification in 2014.

Paul Tovell

Paul is District Manager for Staffordshire County Council. He started his career in Nottinghamshire and is an active member of CILIP Special Interest Groups. He is a national committee member for the Public and Mobile Libraries Group and is corresponding member for the UK of the public library section of the International Federation of Library Associations and Institutions (IFLA).

Keith Trickey

Keith was a senior lecturer at Liverpool Business School and is now a lead trainer for Sherrington Sanders delivering training in cataloguing and classification and personal development. He has coached and mentored for more than 15 years. He is passionate about well-being, diet, cycling and family history.

Margaret Watson

Margaret was President of CILIP in 2003–4; the main theme for her presidency was CPD. She was also chair of CILIP's Qualifications Framework Steering Group and their Ethics Panel. Margaret started in academic libraries before moving to lecturing in 1987, becoming Head of Subject Division and acting Head of Department at Northumbria University. She was a member of the Northern Training Group, based in the North East, for many years and was involved in advanced ICT training for public librarians. Now retired, Margaret works as a consultant and has facilitated training for the CILIP Mentor Scheme.

Sue Westcott

Sue is the Head of Knowledge Management in the Localities Team at the Department of Communities and Local Government (DCLG). She is a CILIP Chartership mentor and a committee member and editor of the Network of Government Library and Information Specialists' journal. She was previously a CILIP councillor, member of the CILIP Executive Board (2000–2005) and Vice Chair of the Government Library and Information Group, and also Secretary of CDL: Heads of Profession for Library and Information Managers.

Ruth Wilkinson

Ruth spent the first 12 years of her career in the hotel and catering industry. After running her own business for five years she decided to have a go at something else and graduated from Northumbria University in 2004 with a first class BSc (Hons) in information and communication management. Her first post was as assistant librarian for a law firm based in Newcastle. In January 2005 she was appointed information specialist at National Building Specification (NBS), and in October 2007 was promoted to Information Services Co-coordinator. Her role involves the delivery of construction industry information products.

Keith Wilson

Keith is the Technical Information Director of RIBA Enterprises Ltd. He has been involved with CILIP professional registration for over 30 years at local regional and national levels, and has been a member of CILIP's Chartership and Accreditation boards. He is a CILIP mentor and chaired the board that steered the development of CILIP's Professional Registration. He has been a CILIP trustee and an external examiner in mathematics and information sciences at Northumbria University.

Foreword

Society, clients and employers have become more demanding and sceptical of the library information and knowledge professional. The increasingly complex and international nature of society, pressures on clients from information overload and scarcity of time, and constantly changing emphases of political, economic, social, technological, legal and environmental (PESTLE) factors on employers are continuing to increase expectations of professional skill and behaviour. Meanwhile accountability of some professionals, lack of transparency, perceived self-interest and examples of poor performance and behaviour in some sectors are being increasingly forcefully reproached by those whom professionals serve.

Nothing less than a guarantee of skills, knowledge and a deep and ethical commitment to engaging with the most difficult, 'wicked' problems is required from clients and stakeholders.

CILIP Members work alongside those belonging to other professional bodies. Many are also members of other professional bodies. Stakeholders hearing the word 'professional' will assume high standards and confident practice irrespective of the particular profession a practitioner belongs to. Proving our right to be a CILIP professional begins with a qualification as the most important indicator of achievement and commitment. It is the start. The professional registration programme supports Members with a range of qualifications and tools to ensure you continue to prove your right to be a CILIP professional.

For some years the Portfolio has been increasingly widely adopted by professions as their main way of assessing applications to practise as a professional. It has been a foundation of CILIP's professional registration programme for a decade. What benefit does this bring to society, clients and employers?

The Portfolio is a record of the journey you have been on to date, including your academic study and training. However, it is much more than this. It is a gallery in which your developing professional inquisitiveness, reflection and personality can be shown. Once you have qualified, it is there to be developed and drawn upon through your career, including when you apply for a higher level of CILIP professional registration. It will help you to plan your professional development, reflect on your professional journey to date, and spot opportunities to exploit and weaknesses to fix.

Your Portfolio will be underpinned by CILIP's Professional Knowledge and Skills Base (PKSB), which in turn defines professional registration. Launched in 2012, the PKSB is the standard used to define what the profession does, the depth to which a practitioner needs to practise at present, and their plans to handle change and development. Together with the Code of Professional Practice and CILIP Ethical Principles it shapes your professional practice.

Most Members starting to plan their Portfolios find it difficult to know where to start. They might question whether they have the right evidence or enough time and resilience to finish the job. It can feel lonely. Help is on hand through CILIP's mentor network. Your mentor's experience and support will be invaluable in giving you the confidence to make your application successful. Your mentor will guide you towards the important questions you will need to ask at all stages in preparing your Portfolio. They will point out other resources including Member networks and interest groups. Once you start asking questions they will help you to answer them for yourself. They are adept at ensuring you take responsibility for planning and delivering your application, because this is an important test of your professional competence.

CILIP mentoring is also an important way for the professional registration programme to develop and assess your approach to reflective practice. The concept of the reflective practitioner was explained by Schön (1983). In FE and HE the Gibbs (1988) reflective cycle is often used as the model when developing understanding of what reflection is and what the outcomes of it are. Reflective skill is now widely expected in all walks of life. Many modern methods of performance, risk analysis and planning – for example critical incident reporting – expect reflection. Most people find that they have to work hard to understand and polish the skills of the reflective practitioner.

Your Portfolio is your opportunity to show what your education, training and work experience have meant and where they have led you. Your journey and reflection on it will build your understanding of the breadth and depth of wider professional issues, not only of your current job but also of the context of library information and knowledge provision for all parts of society.

Once again, CILIP's PKSB provides the practical map of the wide range of skills and knowledge that make up our profession. Most of us need deeper understanding only of some areas of professional expertise. Your Portfolio is an opportunity to reflect upon our profession's ethics and values and explore other areas of interest, current concern and debate in the profession at large. Here you can show a different, more personal side of your understanding of the profession. It is a starting point for a professional obligation, which you will continue throughout your life as a practitioner.

Once built, your Portfolio brings personal benefits apart from providing the means for your professional registration application. Like most professional organizations, CILIP strongly encourages Members to maintain and submit their record of personal professional activity and achievement. This is done through the Members' virtual learning environment (VLE). CILIP's mentor network is also on hand if you require it. Your yearly Revalidation is proof of your commitment to high standards and continuous improvement. In addition your Portfolio becomes a source of reflection, helping you to judge the changes to your knowledge, thinking and practice in the light of change generally. There is evidence (Brine and Feather, 2003) to show that building your Portfolio can improve your ability to understand your development and keep a record of it.

There are a number of ways that you can assess your professional journey and professional development needs. One of the most widely used is by examining strengths, weaknesses, opportunities and threats through a SWOT analysis. It is a useful complement to the PKSB in helping you to identify room for improvement and reinforce your personal confidence and opportunity in areas you excel.

For the time being, however, you are at the stage of building a professional Portfolio. Use the guidance notes and tools available to you through CILIP's VLE. Plan the flow and logic of your material. Organize it. Your mentor is there to guide and support the directions you will decide to take and questions you will need to ask and answer. Share and draw on the experience of colleagues and Members. With everything you put into your Portfolio ask 'what – so what – what next'? You will learn things about yourself in the process that you will use during your career. Stretch yourself, and enjoy those moments when you realize something you did is more important and successful than you thought.

Keith Wilson
Technical Information Director, RIBA Enterprises Ltd

Acknowledgements

My thanks to all those people who have contributed to this third edition both directly through their written contributions and indirectly through discussions and support. My knowledge of this process has been enhanced through my work on the Professional Registration and Accreditation Board where colleagues give their time and expertise freely and generously. Members of the staff team at CILIP are also a mine of information. The earlier editions of this book, written by Margaret Watson, have provided the basis for this new updated edition. Without Margaret's work my task would have been much more difficult.

Kath Owen

I should like to thank all the colleagues who have contributed their personal stories for this book, my friends in the Qualifications and Professional Development Team at CILIP, the marvellous team of mentors, and all the people I have spoken to about CILIP qualifications at various events around the country. Much of the book has been written as a result of those conversations; much of the interest and value is in the personal stories, but any errors are mine. Thanks also to the team at Facet for their help, to Margaret Chapman for her help with the revision, and most of all to Charlie for listening and giving me the space to write.

Margaret Watson

1

Introduction and getting started

The purpose of the book

The Chartered Institute of Library and Information Professionals (CILIP) introduced a professional registration scheme in December 2013. There are four elements in the scheme: Certification, Chartered Membership, Fellowship and Revalidation for Chartered Members and Fellows. The assessment of each level is by submission of an electronic Portfolio. This book has been written to support any Member of CILIP who wishes to apply for professional registration. This third edition reflects the introduction of professional registration and contains some personal contributions. For many of us working in the library and information profession the production of a Portfolio is a new experience and there has been much discussion about the nature of the Portfolio. This book is designed to answer some of those questions, sharing the experience, hints and tips of putting a Portfolio together from colleagues who have successfully achieved professional registration. Some of the contributors have completed their Portfolios very recently using the current regulations, others worked to the old regulations and, as the content requirements are so similar, their experiences are still relevant and a useful source of help for new candidates.

Each chapter deals with a specific aspect of the Portfolio, giving examples from each level as appropriate. The book can be either read straight through by potential candidates or used with greater discretion by applicants who may be having difficulties with particular elements of the Portfolio.

In the Foreword, Keith Wilson provides an overview of how Portfolios can be used in all aspects of a career and how important reflection is for the information professional.

This first chapter is an introductory chapter, looking at the purpose of the book and briefly outlining CILIP's Framework of Qualifications.

It discusses the process of getting started and the support available to Members as they put together their Portfolios, especially the CILIP Mentor Scheme. There are two very important aspects to the Framework: all Portfolios must meet specified assessment criteria, and applicants must demonstrate an appropriate level of reflective writing within their Portfolios. Chapter 2 discusses the assessment criteria and attempts to show how applicants can build their Portfolio to ensure that it meets those criteria; in a case study Keith Wilson, a previous Chair of the Chartership Board, gives his views on assessment. Chapter 3 focuses on working with a mentor, which is required for Certification, Chartership and Fellowship, and includes two case studies. Chapter 4 is concerned with reflective writing and how to begin the habit of reflection and learning to be more evaluative; in a case study Keith Trickey describes his life experience as a reflective writer. Chapters 5 to 8 consider each element of the Portfolio in more detail: the curriculum vitae (CV), the PKSB, the evaluative statement and supporting evidence. Each chapter provides hints and tips about the element it covers and provides personal stories from ACLIPs, MCLIPs and FCLIPs. Finally, in Chapter 9, there is an outline of presentation and submission and some thought is given to what happens next.

All the chapters in this book refer to CILIP's website (www.cilip.org.uk/cilip/jobs-and-careers/qualifications-and-professional-enrolment) and the information and supporting documentation that can be found there. It is essential that you check there for the most up-to-date information and requirements.

Remember, you are not alone in going through this process, and we can learn much from other people's experiences.

Membership of the Professional Register of CILIP

Professional registration is only available to Members of CILIP and is recognized globally. In order to become a Member of CILIP, you should look at the website and follow the instructions for joining.

The next step is to decide which level is appropriate for you:

- Certification
- Chartership
- Fellowship
- Revalidation.

Certification

If you have experience of working in an information role, you can gain recognition for your knowledge, understanding and competence. Certification focuses on demonstrating your knowledge and skills and developing these in the workplace.

Certification is the first step on the professional registration journey and is available to all Members of CILIP. The post-nominals ACLIP are awarded to successful candidates.

Chartership

Achieving Chartership enables you to prove your ability to apply your knowledge and skills in the workplace. You will develop your abilities through learning and reflection and Chartership requires you to provide evidence to demonstrate evaluative and reflective skills relating to your personal performance.

There are no barriers to entry; Chartership is available to all CILIP Members whether they have done Certification or not. The post-nominals MCLIP are awarded to successful candidates.

Fellowship

Fellowship is the highest level of professional registration and if you hold a senior position in your organization or have made a significant contribution to the information professions, this is an appropriate level for you.

Fellowship is a great way to evaluate the impact that you have had in your organization and on the wider profession, and to have your contributions recognized and valued by your peers.

CILIP Membership is the only prerequisite required to undertake Fellowship. The post-nominals FCLIP are awarded to successful candidates.

Revalidation

The way to demonstrate your ongoing commitment to continuing professional development (CPD) is to revalidate your Certification, Chartership or Fellowship.

Having decided which level is right for you, register for that level; you will then be able to access all parts of the website including the VLE and details of how to work towards professional registration.

The Portfolio approach

Building a Portfolio to demonstrate your best work is not a new concept. Artists, photographers and architects have always used this approach and recently more professions, such as the teaching profession, have adopted the Portfolio concept. Your Portfolio is an evaluative review of professional development and should present evidence to demonstrate that you meet the criteria of assessment leading to professional registration. CILIP sets the criteria (see Chapter 2) and each individual applicant selects their own evidence to meet those criteria. CILIP chose the Portfolio approach based on the experience of the Professional Registration and Accreditation Board, CILIP's equivalent of an examination board, over many years and on the increasing need of information professionals to evaluate, articulate and demonstrate their effectiveness and value. If we learn early in our careers to analyse, record and evaluate our professional development as it occurs, then it is easier to plan and engage in CPD.

(Chapter 4 discusses reflective writing in more detail.)

The Portfolio approach allows individuals to present information that they have selected to meet the criteria. The evidence should reflect on a range of professional activities and provide a rounded picture of each applicant, emphasizing what individuals have personally learned: output rather than input. The heart of the Portfolio is not the posts you have held or the courses you have undertaken but the outcome of those activities. The focus is on you and how you have developed professionally and personally to meet the challenges of a demanding and ever-changing information environment. The Portfolio covers past achievements, present experience and proposed development.

The e-Portfolio

The Portfolio which you submit for professional registration will be an e-Portfolio. Information on what it must contain and suggestions for compiling it are on the CILIP website and accessible from the VLE. When you have become a Member of CILIP and have registered for your chosen level, you will be able to access all the information that you need.

Support for Portfolio building

For many of us, compiling a Portfolio is a new experience so, as well as the handbooks and regulations for each level, there are additional sources of support for candidates. CILIP's regional Member networks organize events specifically for candidates and have regional candidate support officers. Much of the support is aimed at Certification and Chartership candidates, but there are also some events for Fellowship and Revalidation candidates. Information on these events is available on the CILIP website, www.cilip.org.uk, under the Jobs and Careers tab.

The Professional Services Team at CILIP can help with individual queries and advise overseas candidates on all aspects of their applications.

There are discussion lists for each level, except Fellowship:

- Certification: LIS-CILIP-ACLIP
- Chartership: LIS-CILIP-REG
- Revalidation: LIS-CILIP-REVAL.

To join any of these discussions lists go to www.jiscmail.ac.uk. These lists allow for frank and down-to-earth discussion between candidates.

Another essential means of support is the CILIP mentor scheme. Lists of mentors and information on becoming a mentor and details of training courses run by CILIP are also available on the website.

It is compulsory for all professional registration candidates to have a mentor. It can be helpful to have a mentor from outside your organization and from a different sector. This helps you to look beyond your job and to see your role in a wider professional context.

Your mentor cannot be your line manager.

Mentoring can take place face to face or in a virtual relationship. Mentor support is crucial for overseas Members. Candidates for Fellowship may choose a mentor from a different profession if they wish, who may be someone with whom the candidate already has a mentoring relationship. A mentor who is registered on the CILIP Mentor Scheme will have undertaken mentor training and be familiar with the process of building a Portfolio. The mentor is not a supervisor but is there to help and support you to select evidence and build the most effective Portfolio.

Many people ask to see examples of successful Portfolios and sometimes the candidate support officers in the regional Member networks can supply these but remember, your Portfolio is unique – it is about you and how you meet the assessment criteria. There is no perfect model Portfolio, just an effective Portfolio demonstrating your development.

2
Assessment criteria

What are assessment criteria?

At its simplest, assessment can be defined as the process whereby evidence of achievement is judged. Each CILIP award recognizes the achievement of the applicant. For professional registration the evidence put forward is the Portfolio. Your Portfolio is assessed by at least two professional colleagues who are members of the Professional Registration and Accreditation Board. It is essential that you become familiar with the particular assessment criteria against which your Portfolio will be judged.

You should keep a copy of the criteria next to your PC or on the desk where you are working on your Portfolio. It is so easy to get carried away by collecting evidence that you can sometimes forget to focus on the criteria. The assessment criteria tell you what you need to demonstrate. Ask yourself frequently whether your Portfolio presents the correct evidence to meet the criteria.

The assessment criteria for each level are discussed in this chapter and broken down to help you ensure that all essential areas are covered. These are followed by reflections on assessment by Keith Wilson. (There are further guidelines for each element of your Portfolio in succeeding chapters.)

Certification (ACLIP)

Identify areas for improvement in personal performance and undertake activities to develop skills and enhance knowledge

Key words and terms:

- identify
- improvement in personal performance
- undertake activities
- develop skills
- enhance knowledge.

Think about your performance at work, what is going well and what you could improve. How can you make improvements, what could you do, on your own or with help from other people?

What sort of activities would help? Possible activities include reading, online or offline, journals or books; watching other people; attending a training event; or just talking to your manager or a colleague.

Your starting point for this is the PKSB (see Chapter 6). This will help you to reflect on your current performance and identify needs for further development. Remember that you will only be working on selected areas that are relevant to your work. An additional aid may be any performance appraisal or development scheme that you already have in your workplace.

You may find it helpful to draw up a plan for your development activities, a simple table will do. This will help you to keep track of what you have done and what you have learned as a result.

When you have completed some activity, think about what skills you have developed or what knowledge you have gained and how you have used this in your work, or how you will use it when the opportunity arises. Add details to your table or write brief notes to summarize your experience.

The table or the notes can form part of your supporting evidence (see Chapter 8).

Consider the organizational context of your service and examine your role within the organization

Key words and terms:

- consider
- organizational context
- examine
- your role.

How does your service fit into the wider organization of which it is a part? It might be a school or college library within the whole school or college, a public library in the context of the whole council or local community, a medical library in the context of a hospital or NHS service, and so on.

What does your service contribute to the wider organization; how does it help the organization to meet its aims and objectives?

How effective is your service? Does it meet its own objectives? What is good, what could be improved and how does your role contribute to service effectiveness?

You do not need to look at everything that your service does; select one or two areas of service effectiveness and reflect on them, perhaps including the results of a user survey or use of statistical evidence to demonstrate your point.

Enhance your knowledge of information services in order to understand the wider professional context within which you work

Key words and terms:

- enhance
- knowledge of information services
- wider professional context.

What do you know about other library and information services? How could you find out more?

Think about visiting other sorts of libraries formally or informally, or talking to people who work in other sectors. You can also learn by reading professional literature and finding out about issues that affect the profession.

Some brief notes about what you have learned and how your learning could be relevant to your work will form part of your supporting evidence.

If your mentor works in a different sector they may be able to help you plan a visit or discuss their area of work. They can also discuss issues that you have read about, but give them advance warning so they can do some reading too!

Chartership (MCLIP)

Identify areas for improvement in your personal performance, undertake activities to develop skills, apply them in practice, and reflect on the process and outcomes

Key words and terms:

- identify
- improvement in personal performance
- undertake activities
- develop skills
- apply in practice
- reflect on process and outcomes.

The first criterion is about being a reflective practitioner, thinking about what you have done in the workplace in the last one or two years, what you have achieved, what you wish to improve and how you intend to do this. You should also reflect on what you have learned from the activities you have undertaken and how you have put your learning into practice.

Using the PKSB (Chapter 6) will help you to identify your skills gaps. Workplace performance appraisal or staff development schemes may help. You can also discuss this with your line manager and your mentor to identify appropriate development activities and opportunities to undertake them.

You may find it helpful to draw up a plan for your development activities; a simple table will do. This will help you to keep track of what you have done and what you have learned as a result.

When you have completed an activity, think about what skills you have developed or what knowledge you have gained, and how you have used this in your work or how you will use it when the opportunity arises. This can also be part of your table, or you may wish to write some brief notes to reflect on your experience.

The table or the notes can form part of your supporting evidence (see Chapter 8).

Examine the organizational context of your service, evaluate service performance, show the ability to implement or recommend improvement, and reflect on actual or desired outcomes

Key words and terms:

- examine
- organizational context of your service
- evaluate
- service performance
- implement or recommend improvement
- reflect
- actual or desired outcomes.

These criteria require you to apply all your reflective skills to examine, evaluate and reflect on service performance and to express your views on its effectiveness. You are required to consider your service in the context of the wider organization; for example, a college library as part of the whole college, or a legal information service in a large private company. Look at your service aims and objectives and make your own judgement about how effectively they are met and how effectively your service contributes to the whole organization. It is perfectly acceptable to criticize the organization for which you work, as long as you do so constructively and fairly.

Are there any improvements which would help the service? Explain how you would implement them if you are able to do so, or make recommendations on how they could be made. Reflect on actual or desired outcomes and the differences they would make to performance.

Incorporate a copy of the service aims and objectives (or a selected extract from them) in your evidence. This may include annotations, or your comments in a separate document. If your organization does not have any aims or objectives, consider what you would include if you were asked to draw them up; write down your thoughts and reflect on how effectively the organization meets the notional aims and objectives, and what could be improved, as suggested above.

Your own or others' surveys and statistical information can provide useful evidence for this criterion; think about and write notes about your personal conclusions about how the information gained can be used to help your service, which you can include in your evidence.

Enhance your knowledge of the wider professional context and reflect on areas of current interest

Key words and terms:

- enhance
- knowledge of the wider professional context
- reflect
- areas of current interest.

The evidence you include for this criterion should show that you can see beyond your workplace and sector and have an understanding of the wider profession and the issues and concerns that it faces.

You may achieve this understanding through professional reading of journals, blogs or books; discussions with colleagues or your mentor; visits to other information providers or settings; involvement in CILIP groups or regional Member networks; or attendance at conferences or events.

Your evidence should include your reflections on some of these activities; express your views on professional matters clearly.

Fellowship (FCLIP)

Identify areas for improvement in personal performance, undertake activities to develop skills, apply them in practice, and reflect on the process and outcomes

This criterion requires you to use the PKSB and any other appropriate workplace experience to reflect on your CPD. You could consider your personal and professional development in your career to date, or make a 'before and after' assessment against the PKSB based on a particular section of your career. It is essential that you demonstrate an active commitment to CPD and can reflect on what you have gained from it.

Examine the organizational context of your work and evidence substantial achievement in professional practice

The key words in this criterion are 'substantial achievement'. This achievement may be in your workplace or sector, or in the wider context of the information profession. Thus it may be based on seniority within an organization, a position of influence within a group or committee, or a particular piece of work or research. You should reflect on how this achievement has been reached and what makes it 'substantial' in your view.

Establish your commitment to, and enhance your knowledge of, the information profession in order to have made a significant contribution to all or part of it

The key words in this criterion are 'significant contribution'. You should reflect on the impact that your knowledge and skills have had, which is likely to be beyond your organization. You may have carried out research or developed a piece of work which you have shared with the wider profession through conference papers or publication. You may have been or still be involved in activities for CILIP or a specialist group, which have contributed to professional development or learning.

Even more than for other levels of professional registration, every submission for Fellowship will be very different, as experienced practitioners will come from a wide range of sectors, with varying degrees of specialism. Your Portfolio should contain a great deal of analysis and reflection on your career to date. It must be much more than a description of your career, which should be covered in your CV. Each applicant chooses their own themes on which to focus the Portfolio, but the evidence must meet the criteria.

Revalidation

Revalidation is available for all Members of CILIP; it provides a formal way to record your CPD. Most regulated professions in the UK have compulsory Revalidation in response to the dynamic changes facing all professionals in the workplace. Many information professionals follow CPD programmes to enhance their knowledge, skills and expertise, and CILIP is seeking to record that achievement.

All candidates must demonstrate that they have:

- spent a minimum of 20 hours per year on personal and professional development
- reflected on how development activities have contributed to their professional practice for the level being revalidated (maximum 250 words)
- recorded evidence on a CPD log provided on the CILIP VLE (see Chapter 6), or using an alternative format for recording the CPD if, for example, the workplace has a system in place which covers the same ground.

Assessment of CILIP professional registration

The assessment of CILIP professional registration is carried out by the Professional Registration and Accreditation Board. Dates of board meetings can be found on the CILIP website.

CILIP Professional Registration and Accreditation Board

The Professional Registration and Accreditation Board is made up of volunteers from a range of sectors who are experienced information professionals. They meet four times a year to discuss applications. Each Portfolio is normally assessed by two board members and then, in the case of rejection, by a moderator, who is also a member of the board. Should there then be disagreement among the three assessors so that two recommend rejection and the third person feels it should be accepted, the application goes to all board members for discussion and a final decision at their next meeting. Periodic e-meetings are held to speed the processing of applications which are judged to be acceptable by both assessors. CILIP appoints two external examiners to monitor the work of the Board and to ensure that procedures are followed correctly.

Hints and tips

- Read the criteria carefully at the beginning of the process.
- Keep a copy of the assessment criteria on your desk or at the front of your Portfolio file.
- Make sure that the evidence in your Portfolio demonstrates how you meet the criteria.
- Give your Portfolio to a mentor or critical friend to proofread and check against the criteria.
- The assessors can only assess what is put before them, so make sure that your Portfolio includes all necessary elements and meets the assessment criteria.

CASE STUDY 2.1
Keith Wilson: The criteria of assessment – why have them?

CILIP's four levels of recognition of personal professional achievement provide a flexible framework for library and information service workers to extend and modernize their knowledge and skills, and for this progression to be recognized in formal professional qualifications. Central to this process is the submission from the applicant of evidence for assessment, making the case for professional registration. The process involves a number of professional and administrative colleagues and is open to independent scrutiny. Assessment of applications needs to be rigorous, fair, transparent and supportive.

A standardized question-and-answer examination is inappropriate for many reasons, including inability to accommodate the increasing diversity of work that CILIP Members do; differences in the evidence applicants would prefer to use to make a case; development of the evidence-based profession; and opportunity to emphasize information that applicants feel will reinforce their case. Question-and-answer examinations concentrate on outputs. The Portfolio solves these issues, and enables standards to be maintained and professional registration to be developed through experience and changing circumstance.

How do applicants know what is expected? How do applicants and assessors know what is and is not acceptable? How do those outside of the profession judge the value of registered Members? Standards for evaluation provide the answer, known as the criteria of assessment. These have nothing to do with making sure that applicants submit the right paperwork (although this is important); they indicate what needs to be done to ensure that an application is acceptable, and they help to achieve thoroughness, consistency and fairness. They are concerned with outcome, the personal professional progression that makes and will make a difference in the applicant's workplace, to the wider community and to themselves. They also provide the means by which others can judge the value of standards set for CILIP professional registration. How do the criteria affect those involved in the process?

Applicants and assessment criteria

Although emphasis and expectations differ according to the level applicants are applying for, three broad objectives form the backbone to the criteria:

1   Be able to critically evaluate: this goes hand in glove with the ability to reflect on professional experience and knowledge, constantly

reassessing need and opportunity in the light of the organization and the changing world in which it and applicants work. This objective provides applicants with the means to demonstrate professional judgement, maturity, knowledge and expertise.

2 Understand the importance of being up to date with professional development and practice and demonstrate practical application. This enables applicants to show how they are equipped to deal with change, sharing and implementing practice from, and dealing with, issues of concern to the wider profession.

3 Reflect on personal performance: applicants can make the case for the extent to which they have fused ability, skills and knowledge, demonstrating how they have changed, and what difference they expect this will make in their future career and to their contribution to the profession at large.

These objectives overlay CILIP's body of PKSB. Applicants must meet all criteria for their chosen level. An application will not be accepted if one criterion is not met.

The Professional Registration and Accreditation Board and assessment criteria

The Professional Registration and Accreditation Board judges only what is presented by the applicant. Although there is an expectation that applicants will have carefully proofread their applications, and that they are well organized, these aspects are not included in the criteria of assessment. Specified word counts and types of evidence are, however. If assessors are made aware of issues such as nationality, first language or disability, these are taken into account as they may shape the approach the candidate has taken in presenting evidence. Assessment is then made against the criteria of assessment set out in the professional registration handbooks.

Assessors look for objectivity, understanding of role and contribution in the workplace, attention to professional development and demonstration of its value, synthesis of knowledge and experience, and an indication of how all may change or develop in future. Often when mapping evidence to the criteria they will ask 'so what?' or 'why?' If the answer is not clear there is a weakness in the application. Where there is weakness or omission, the assessors may ask the applicant to supply additional information. They base their requirements on the criteria, with a question designed to help the applicant review the application against the criteria.

When the board agrees that an application should be rejected, the reasons are always based on the criteria. An explanation of the decision is always accompanied by supporting guidance from the board.

Where the assessors offer suggestions to successful applicants for further development, they are based on the criteria, and may be accompanied also by suggestions for ways in which future Portfolios may better meet the requirements.

Experience and expertise is shared within the board during the assessment process and generally, and is reflected in regular reviews of procedure. Assessment criteria help to avoid subjective judgements.

External examiners and moderators

The Board's external examiners provide an independent viewpoint and ensure that the Board is thorough, fair and objective. They also help ensure that the criteria for the Open University credit transfer scheme are met. Without the criteria of assessment it would be impossible for the examiners to be confident that standards were being met. The examiners' annual report to the CILIP Council is based on the success of the whole assessment process in achieving consistency against the criteria.

Mentors

The role of the mentor in helping towards a focused application cannot be overestimated. Support, guidance, confidence-building and encouragement from an experienced mentor can always be seen in successful applications. The mentor provides a bridge between the criteria and the mentee's perceptions, and can be very effective in helping the mentee avoid submitting what amounts to simply a descriptive application, the most common reason for rejection. CILIP mentors' main task is to support applicants in preparing their applications; without the assessment criteria this task would be unstructured and it would be very difficult to identify lasting personal benefits that will result from the partnership.

Candidate support officers and assessment criteria

Workshops for professional registration are organized by candidate support officers who are part of the regional Member network structure and the assessment criteria form a central element of them. All candidates and mentors should therefore understand the importance of meeting the assessment criteria.

Conclusion

The criteria of assessment are the building blocks of the professional registration. They ensure consistent and high standards, and provide the means by which personal and professional skills, knowledge and abilities can be assessed. Criteria enable those judging the value of CILIP professional registration to understand the capabilities, capacity and contribution that certificated and Chartered Members can make to organizations and communities.

3
Working with a mentor

Finding a mentor

All candidates for Certification, Chartership and Fellowship are required to have a mentor. Mentors for Certification and Chartership must be on the CILIP Register of Mentors and must be Chartered Members of CILIP. A Fellowship candidate may choose a mentor from outside CILIP if they wish; some may already have a mentor with whom they have worked for some time and who is willing to continue in this role to support an application for Fellowship.

CILIP maintains a register of mentors who have attended training on professional registration. This ensures that they are up to date with the current requirements of professional registration, which will often be slightly different from the regulations under which the mentors themselves completed Chartership. Candidates can approach mentors on the register to ask if they are willing to mentor them. Some candidates may know a registered mentor who is willing to work with them. Candidates are strongly advised to find a mentor who works in a different sector from them. This enables candidates to see their work from a different perspective and to gain a wider view of the profession through discussion and possible visits to a different working environment.

It is not appropriate for your mentor to be your line manager. Working with a mentor should allow the candidate to benefit from the knowledge and experience of someone who is at least one step and preferably several steps away from their day-to-day work environment. Meetings with a mentor should focus on the professional development and views of the candidate without getting tied into or side tracked by the job role and the demands of the organization.

Mentoring does not have to involve face-to-face meetings. It can take place online using Skype, e-mail or any other communication system. It can also take place by phone. This can often help candidates who are based in remote places, who are solo workers, who do not have opportunities to leave the workplace for a meeting, who are based in areas where there are few registered mentors, or who work overseas. For many candidates, and indeed mentors, this may be a new way of working and may take a little time to get used to. It can be very successful.

If you cannot find a mentor from the register, you should contact your regional Member network or the professional registration team at CILIP who will be able to help you.

At your first 'meeting' with your mentor you should complete the mentoring agreement form so that you each know what to expect from the other and how long you expect the relationship to last.

The role of a mentor

> Mentoring is an approach to people development that is independent of and takes place outside any line management responsibility.
>
> Kay and Hinds (2009)

A mentor can take many roles for different candidates. Some candidates need someone to discuss the assessment criteria, to help them to identify the key requirements and then to help the candidate tease out what they have done to demonstrate that they meet the criteria. This often involves helping the candidate to accept that it is OK to praise themselves and to talk about achievements. Many of us are too modest about recognizing what we have done.

It is often helpful to work through the PKSB (see Chapter 6) and to discuss identified gaps with your mentor. A mentor may be able to suggest ways of filling those gaps and later discuss how successful that has been.

Setting a timetable with a mentor with deadlines and stepping stones on the way to completion helps many candidates keep on track and, if necessary, nudges them to complete the application. It is the candidate's responsibility to set this up, to keep to time and to do the work, but for those of us who work well to deadlines, having someone else to encourage, support and even cajole can be very useful. Some mentors worry that candidates are not keeping to their own timetable or go quiet for long periods of time. It is the candidate's responsibility to make their application and to ask for support when needed. Everyone finds themselves in a position at some time when they have been unrealistic in their expectations of themselves, or when circumstances – personal or professional – have conspired to cause changes in working practice. This is normal and may result in moved deadlines. Clearly it is courteous to keep in touch with your mentor so they know what is happening.

All levels of professional registration require candidates to understand the wider professional context in which they work. A mentor can often help by discussing or explaining current issues raised locally or in the professional press. If you wish to discuss a current issue or matter of concern with your mentor, please give them some notice so that they can prepare. Neither mentors nor candidates are expected to be an expert on everything! A mentor may also be able to suggest places to visit so that candidates can see at first hand how services work in a different sector, make their own evaluative comments, and look at practices which they could suggest for their own workplace.

An important role for a mentor is to be a critical friend. This may involve looking at evidence that the candidate has gathered or reading evaluative comments and assessing how well they meet the criteria. This can often result in making suggestions for ideas which could be included or suggestions for editing out description. The candidate must be clear about what they want from their mentor and listen to advice given. However, it will not be your mentor who makes the final assessment (even if your mentor is a member of the Professional

Registration and Accreditation Board) when you submit your application. They can only advise and give their views; the final result of the formal assessment may be different. It is the candidate's decision what is included, what is left out and how it looks. Your mentor cannot make decisions for you.

Having a mentor gives the candidate a rare opportunity to seek someone else's views in a focused way, to benefit from the experience of someone else from a different background and to get an independent view of their work. This is a valuable part of the process from which both mentor and mentee can benefit.

The Mentor of the Year Award is made each year by CILIP to a mentor nominated by their mentee. The winning nomination in 2014 said:

> He has a very relaxed and considerate manner which creates an
> atmosphere where I feel comfortable in voicing my thoughts and opinions.
> . . . Following our discussions I always feel motivated and enthusiastic
> about my professional development and the profession at large.

Many mentors who give their time to support candidates aspire to creating this sort of atmosphere. However, if you or your mentor decides that the relationship is not working or is not beneficial, note that there is information on how to change mentors available on the CILIP website. This may also be useful if personal or professional circumstances change and the mentor can no longer continue in their role.

Mentor–mentee completion form

This form must be included in your Portfolio. It should be completed by the mentor and the mentee and gives the opportunity to reflect on and evaluate the mentor–mentee relationship. Each has a maximum of 250 words to do this.

The mentor is required to write one of the letters of support for Fellowship candidates. Letters of support are not required for Certification or Chartership Portfolios.

CASE STUDY 3.1
Lesley Randall: The value of mentoring

Through the mentoring process I developed as a professional practitioner, gaining knowledge and experience that I could not have acquired elsewhere. Having a mentor working in a different sector at the British Library was very important, allowing for the cross-fertilization of ideas, networking and a sharing of information. My mentor's network enabled me to expand my contacts and organize meetings and take responsibility for my development. My mentor supported me through Chartership, too, and our meetings were invaluable for focused discussions, where I began to lead, reflect and evaluate. This gave me the confidence and experience to reflect critically on my personal performance and be more engaged with evaluating service performance.

CASE STUDY 3.2
Donna Gundry and Nicola Forgham-Healey: Mentoring online
Mentoring online

With the advent of different online resources, such as Skype, Google hangouts, WebEx and Apple's Facetime, it is possible for Chartership candidates to be supported and mentored in a virtual world. Nicola Forgham-Healey and Donna Gundry give an overview of how they found their experience of virtual Chartership mentoring, and insights from others who have ventured online.

There are a variety of reasons why you might like to try this method:

- difficulty finding a mentor in your area
- to avoid using annual leave in order to meet
- because you work in a small team or as a solo librarian, so it is difficult to arrange time off
- to obtain Chartership in your own time
- to save travel costs, as it limits the cost of travel to meet
- to reduce the amount of paper used.

Virtual mentoring removes all of these problems as it allows you to be flexible and you can easily plan calls whenever it suits you. This was one of the main reasons why we undertook virtual or online mentoring. We both work in very busy (academic and health) libraries, and struggled to find the time during the day to catch up and discuss any issues. A geographical reason was that we live over 200 miles apart and meeting was going to be problematic. These were the main reasons why we decided to use an online method of communication. We chose Skype as it was easy to install on computers and iPads and we had previous knowledge of using it. We held our meetings in the evening, in the comfort of our homes, as this was the easiest way to meet.

During a Chartership Twitter chat, we mentioned that we were communicating via Skype, and an interesting conversation occurred as another Chartership candidate wondered how this would work. This was one of the reasons why we wanted to share our experiences with others. We were interested in finding out if any other mentors or mentees have used this method so we created a survey and sent it to various discussion lists – our aim was to find out if others had had the same experiences as we had.

We found that online communication was being used by others, in order for people separated by distance and time to communicate for virtual mentoring, for example:

> Online communication is the best way to ensure communication with international candidates (one of my mentees is based in the USA, another in Africa).

We used Skype, and others have used a number of different packages. Figure 3.1 shows the online systems used for virtual mentoring. The most popular are Skype and +Google as they can easily be downloaded on a mobile device or a computer.

One system used for online mentoring is Wiggio (http://wiggio.com/), which allows users to hold virtual meetings, send texts and share folders. We will investigate this in future as it seems to put all of the information in one place.

One respondent to our survey had used WebEx:

> I mentored a candidate in Cornwall when I am based in North Yorkshire. There was no way we could meet, but we found using telephone and email worked fine

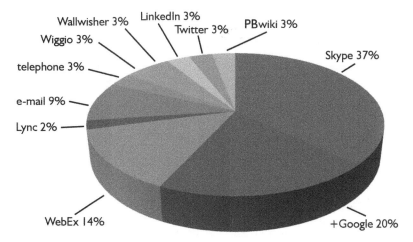

Wallwisher 3% LinkedIn 3% PBwiki 3%
Wiggio 3% Twitter 3%
telephone 3%
Skype 37%
e-mail 9%
Lync 2%

WebEx 14% +Google 20%

Figure 3.1 Online systems used for virtual mentoring

for us. We also used Facebook a little. I've used WebEx in other contexts and I think it's good once you get used to it, if you need to involve more than 2 people.

Table 3.1 lists the pros and cons of various virtual tools.

Mentor's experience

This was the first time that I had used Skype in this context, having previously only used it to talk to friends and family. Having mentored other candidates I was used to meeting and discussing issues and queries face to face. I was interested in using Skype to see how it compared. I will admit that I found it strange at first, partly because body language is limited and there were times when it was difficult to get the conversation flowing – although this is eased with having an agenda to work through.

It was very useful being able to share documents online using WeTransfer (https://www.wetransfer.com/), so we did not need to store and send large documents via e-mail. This could be a useful way of saving paper, but I found it easier to print out the information and have it in front of me. In some ways I have found this method of communicating a lot easier than meeting face to face, as I was at home, cup of tea in front of me; in a way it has been more relaxing as I have not had to travel anywhere.

Table 3.1 Pros and cons of various virtual tools

Virtual tool	How to access	Accessible via	Overall view
CILIP VLE	Easy to log in; there are various tutorials available on how to use it.	Internet	Option to share Chartership page with mentor who can directly comment on the work undertaken; makes it easier to edit and comment on documents without having to send large documents via e-mail.
Facetime	As long as have Apple phone and telephone number or e-mail, just like a telephone call but can see person at the end of phone.	iPad, iPhone	Very similar to Skype; able to see other person's reactions so can easily read their body language.
Google Hangouts	Need Google account. Very easy to use; can either download the app, or install it onto computer. Computer needs a webcam in order to get the most benefit.	Desktop computer, iPad, iPhone	Important to know handle name of other people 'hanging out' with so able to find them before call. Works very much like FaceTime and Skype.
Skype	Very easy to set up an account and to access, although needs a webcam and microphone.	Desktop computer, iPad, iPhone, Android	Very easy to use once set up, and suitable time to meet is agreed.
WebEx	Need a subscription to access. Advisable to test program before main meeting, to iron out any problems.	iPhone, iPad, desktop computer	Very good for sharing documents and discussions; it can use any webcam on device.

I have also found that because I was at home I was able to be more candid as I was out of a work environment; it was easier to discuss any issues or problems without the worry of anyone overhearing us. Also we stuck to a tight time-frame. There have been some technical issues; one meeting had to be abandoned as the wi-fi connection was lost, and during some conversations the connection was slow, but we have persevered using this method.

We have used e-mail and the odd telephone call when Donna was close to submitting her Portfolio. I think that if we had not been using Skype, I would have found the distance too hard and I would not have been able to mentor her. Skype has been invaluable, and I would use it again in future.

Mentee's experience

Skype was not something I had previously used, but I was aware of the possible benefits. I wouldn't say I was reluctant but I was not embracing the technology either – I was somewhere in between. I was concerned that the technology and image quality of the system was not going to be good enough for a sustainable conversation. However, after the first session it became clear that using Skype was more suitable for our conversations than meeting in person. My mentor used a computer, while I started with a laptop and moved on to my iPad.

Cons: we were limited by time delay in conversation; we needed another system to send documents (https://www.wetransfer.com/); we needed to adjust lighting of the rooms we were in to see the other person clearly. However, after the first two or three sessions, this was less noticeable and could easily be resolved. During the two years we faced very few technical problems.

Pros: there was no travel time or connected costs; free software; using Skype made explaining elements much easier than using e-mail. Overall it was much cheaper to use Skype than travelling to meet, especially when some of the meetings were only 30 minutes long. Image quality was respectable, but depended on lighting and camera movement.

Our top tips for mentoring online

1   Agree a time and a method of communicating in case either one of you forgets – this happened once.
2   Before you have your first meeting, arrange a quick test of the equipment, as without it you are not going to get very far!
3   Agree the length of time you are going to have the meeting; this is important as you are using your free time.
4   Use an online storage system such as Dropbox (https://www.dropbox.com/) or WeTransfer (https://www.wetransfer.com/). These are very useful ways of sharing documents, though you may not be able to access them at work.
5   We have found an agenda works very well as it helps you keep to the point and go through the information quickly.

6   Be prepared for weather disruptions – we have been cut off because of a bad thunderstorm.

7   Using Skype does not always work so if necessary be honest and use telephones and e-mails.

Useful websites

*   CILIP VLE: http://vle.cilip.org.uk/
*   DropBox: https://www.dropbox.com/
*   WeTransfer: https://www.wetransfer.com/

To conclude, we would like to end by quoting another mentor who sums up online mentoring perfectly:

> I'd gladly use online communication for future mentoring – it opens up so many options! I think it will become more popular as people start looking to find the right mentor, no matter where they're based. It can also help people who have time constraints, as it removes the need to travel (even a short distance) and helps to keep you more focussed on business, so meetings are shorter.

4

Reflective writing

What is reflective writing?

Reflective writing is the formal or informal recording of your thoughts. Reflective practice requires that you learn from your practical professional experience (Booth and Brice, 2004). So first we have to learn to reflect on our learning and professional practice, and then we have to become accustomed to recording that reflection in writing. By recording the reflection we formalize the process and have a record of our development.

If you Google 'reflective writing' you will find many useful and interesting ideas to help you get started. Remember that your thoughts and therefore the recording of those thoughts are personal to you and different from the more academic writing that you may be more used to.

Many of us find it difficult to write reflectively; like most skills, though, the more practice you have, the easier it becomes.

Reflective practice

Those of you who are fans of Harry Potter will remember a wonderful magical object that Albus Dumbledore owned called the pensieve. Professor Dumbledore could place memories into this stone basin and then relive them, taking Harry with him so he could learn from those memories. This is a good example of reflection and underscores the importance of learning from experience. It is not sufficient to just have an experience; reflect on that experience and evaluate it, and then apply that knowledge to another experience or activity. Deep and sustained learning – becoming able to do something you could not do before – only comes through experience, but experience on its own is not enough. Experience needs to be reflected on and made sense of to create knowledge, and this knowledge deepened when it is applied in fresh situations (Thomson, 2006).

So before reflective writing comes reflection. As part of your CPD you should try to get into the habit of being reflective – thinking about the task you have just performed, the course you have been on, the discussion you have just had at work, the article you have just read, and so on. Any activity that is part of your working life should be reflected on, and lessons learned. Keith Trickey reveals later in this chapter that reflection can also become a part of your personal development as well as your professional development.

Evaluation

Most of us are familiar with evaluation forms, often handed out at the end of workshops. Distributing evaluation forms at workshops enables the leader to reflect on the success or otherwise of that particular session and plan any improvements for future events. Sometimes people feel that they are suffering from evaluation fatigue, as at the end of each event or workshop they are given another evaluation form to complete. But for presenters and people planning such events they are an important element in planning or revising future programmes. As a presenter it is also useful to try to carry out one's own evaluation, by recording feelings about the elements in the programme – what went well or what could have been done better. If colleagues were involved in different sessions, then they can add their feedback. The personal evaluation, colleagues' feedback, participants' feedback and other evidence (reading or courses attended) all contribute to reflecting on the event and, hopefully, improving future events.

An advantage of completing an evaluation for someone else is that it encourages you to reflect on an event from the presenter's perspective; at the same time, you can jot down your reflections from your perspective. It is a good idea to develop this habit.

The learning cycle

Most writers on reflective practice refer to Kolb's (1986) model of experiential learning. This is normally represented as a learning cycle although it could also be seen as a learning spiral, or simply:

- You do something.
- You think about it.
- You draw conclusions from the experience.
- You plan how you can do it better.
- You do it better.

When you write reflectively remember the three Ws:

- *What?* (a brief description): What happened?
- *So what?* (interpretation): What is the most relevant or important aspect of the event or experience? How does it relate to other experiences?
- *What next?* (outcome): What have I learned? How will I use my learning in the future? What will I do differently next time?

This is what we should ask ourselves all the time. What have I learned from this activity and what am I going to do as a result? This forms the basis of being a reflective practitioner.

Keeping a learning or activity log

There are many ways of keeping a log and you must decide what suits your needs and style of working best. By getting into the habit of reflecting regularly you will have an invaluable source of material for your application and evidence which is easily accessible for your Portfolio.

You can keep a log or diary and complete short entries each day, or perhaps use a weekly diary. Don't just describe or list what happened though. Ask yourself questions (as in the learning cycle above); if possible talk to other people and get their perspective; collect evidence if appropriate.

You could use a blog or other electronic medium to record your reflections and use extracts as examples of reflective writing as well as a personal aide memoire.

Reflective writing for your Portfolio

The personal statement in your Portfolio is clearly the place where you are required to reflect on your learning and development. You are expected not just to describe what you have done, but to analyse any developmental activity, reflect on the outcomes of that activity and consider how you might apply, or have already applied, what you have learned back in the workplace. So before you write your personal statement you have to reflect. If you have tried to start the process as a reflective practitioner from the time you registered it will be so much easier. If you have kept a learning log or a diary, you will have evidence of development, so it will be relatively straightforward to use your reflections as the basis for your personal statement.

A daily routine

To start the process get into the habit of reviewing any developmental activity and recording your feelings. You can then add a record of discussion with other people and notes from books, reports and articles that you have read on the subject. There are many ways in which you can incorporate reflective writing into your daily routine:

- If you give a presentation, evaluate it; ask colleagues, formally or informally, for their opinions; record how you felt and what you would do differently on another occasion.

- If you go on a visit, record your ideas and note how you could apply anything you saw in your place of work.
- If you go on a training course, make a note of how useful it was and what skills you were able to apply in the workplace.
- Use the CPD audit sheet on CILIP's website.
- Keep an annotated diary, blog or weekly journal.

It is important to make a record as soon as you can after an event and not to rely on memory, but it is also crucial that you revisit and review that record at a later date, making a note of any subsequent developments or feelings. It sounds a huge task but, as Keith Trickey points out in the case study that follows, it should become second nature after a while.

This record of self-evaluation and analysis will be a personal record and you are not expected to share it with anyone else, although you may wish to discuss it with your mentor in order to clarify your thoughts.

The record will ultimately provide you with a wonderful source of information for your Portfolio. When you come to start compiling it, much of the hard work will have been done. You will have a record of your reflection on all aspects of your development and significant amounts of supporting evidence, leaving only the task of selecting and organizing the material that best demonstrates that you meet the assessment criteria.

Hints and tips

- At the end of the day or week record any substantial learning or developmental activity.
- Discuss the activity with a colleague or mentor and make a note of any interesting points.
- Collect any supporting material such as handouts, agendas, flyers, programmes and so forth.
- Use the CILIP audit sheet.
- Keep any memos, letters or feedback on your performance.

- Keep any relevant survey results but add your notes.
- Be honest with yourself.
- Set a realistic time aside to reflect.
- Use travelling time to record your reflections.
- Record your reflections in a diary or make sure that you number the records in some way.
- Revisit and review the entries but don't change them; add thoughts if necessary.

CASE STUDY 4.1
Keith Trickey: Approaches to reflective writing

Sitting down to write is always a very self-conscious act because of the formality involved in presenting our thoughts as text. The conventions of sentence structure and grammar can be ignored in the spoken word, as that huge range of ancillary activity – intonation and gesture – can happily clarify meaning. In text the words themselves have to carry the full weight of the communication, and this is the case whether you work with a pen or a keyboard. So what is the advantage of writing in reflection and how is it best practised?

I will briefly review written reflection from the broad perspective of reflection as a personal development activity, not simply as a required element in professional development. In my experience professional development is simply one aspect in the complex of activities that keeps an individual moving forward to engage in their life in all its varied aspects. What works in the general case also works, helpfully, in that specific pocket of development named professional development.

Daily 'mind dump'

The most unstructured form of reflective writing is what Julia Cameron (1997) refers to as 'pages' and involves a regular commitment (for as long as is still proving useful) to produce two or three sides of written A4 each morning (yes, every morning) as a 'mind dump' to allow you to deal with whatever you need to deal with before you start your day. The discipline of sitting each morning to write is really helpful. Sometimes your thoughts sprint out, enabling you to produce sheets of writing in a matter of minutes – your hand struggling to keep up with your racing mind. Sometimes it is 'with painful steps and slow' that the text drags itself out from under the pen; often these sessions provide very helpful information on how you are and what you need to do. The purpose of 'pages' is self-contained. You simply write, and notice as you write what you write (the content) and how you write (emotional element); there is no requirement to move beyond this as the in-process reflection can be carried forward and your mind cleared to allow you to be more effective for the rest of the day.

I used this method for about three years and during that time it proved very useful in giving me insight and clarity about the competing pressures I was dealing with and in enabling me to work more effectively through the day. At the moment I do not do 'pages'. When I need to I will start again – and stop again when they have served their purpose.

Focused writing

A different approach to reflective writing is offered by Joyce Chapman (1991). Her approach pushes the reflective element more to the fore. Initially there is the requirement to write about something specific in whatever way is appropriate. You could write a series of well articulated lucid paragraphs, a short poem, or a series of anguished bullet points – all in CAPITAL LETTERS to show your passion! The style you adopt should mirror the task you are undertaking. If it is about your relationship with somebody else, it may be helpful to write it as a dialogue, allowing you to explore the other person's voice. Having completed your writing you then leave a space, because you will be coming back to it later. After a couple of days you re-read the passage and then write a feedback statement to yourself. In reading what you have written you take the role of a supportive friend, and it is with that view that you write the feedback, giving a different perspective on the initial writing. I enjoyed this approach to reflective writing as it allows you to move into the mentor role and be self-nurturing, as opposed to being your most powerful critic.

The 'three whats?' tool

If you need to deal with an incident or issue quickly and get some broader thinking around it, then it is helpful to use the 'three whats?' tool (Rolfe, Freshwater and Jasper, 2001). The three basic components to the approach are asking the three questions 'what?', 'so what?' and 'now what?' The first 'what?' basically questions what has happened. This is followed by asking 'so what?' Here the significance of the incident is worked out to see where it fits in the larger picture of your development. For example, the 'what?' – perhaps asking permission to attend a professional development event without having to take leave – may not sound earth shattering, but by asking 'so what?' you might note that it is the first time that you have asked your organization to support you in this way – having previously taken leave when attending such events. That indicates a significant shift in self-valuing in the workplace and it is important that you notice it. Now you can move on to asking 'now what?' This gives the action-centred and future focus to your reflection. So what will this change (now acknowledged) enable you to do (differently) in the future? This allows you to consider future possibilities from the secure basis of acknowledged development.

Self-development through reflective writing

I have always found writing a fascinating process, as it allows me to gain a much more useful perspective on my thinking when I can see it written out on a page. This is a powerful advantage for reflective work. When ideas and thoughts are buzzing around in your head they bump into each other and can easily be hijacked or crushed by the continuous activity of thought. When you write about them you have to focus on specific concerns and give them your attention; also, when those thoughts or issues are expressed on paper they take on a more solid reality, which has a certain separation from your thought process. You can then literally change your mind as you review what you have written. If you write in a slightly self-conscious way about something you have achieved, when you read it through you can simply acknowledge that you have done a good job: this can loop back to build your self-efficacy and expectation around further potential. Without capturing this as text, this possibility for self-development could be lost, as your old view of self continues, failing to acknowledge the professional progress you have made.

If you keep your reflective writing in an A4 notebook and watch it accumulate over a period of time (in my case a series of books covering about ten years) it becomes a useful resource, a way of tracking progress, providing insights on developments and unhelpful habits that are still being worked on.

Dipping into my archive I found the following back in February 1998. I had been through a very rough day at work and in my personal life. I had then travelled to London because I was delivering training the next day. In the early evening I set and answered a brief series of questions:

- Was I 'suffering'? – Yes, I was feeling hurt and neglected.
- Was it useful? – Yes, it opened further areas for consideration.
- Did I end up damaged? – No, I kept things going.
- Did I 'die' of it? – No, it was not that important.

Two hours later I added the simple feedback statement: 'We survived!'

The reflective process worked by overstating my sense of the situation; it allowed my natural humour and playful irony to kick in and clear things.

Reflective writing did not come easily to me – my degree was in English literature, I have always been fascinated with language and I had become expert at hiding behind words, so I could spin elegant text which flashed and impressed but actually had no reflective value. I failed to engage honestly with the topic to hand and instead built an elegant mask with the effort going into the creation of an accomplished piece of writing rather than honestly exploring my condition.

It may take time to find your voice or range of voices in reflective writing, but that simply requires patience and practice. Approached with a healthy curiosity about the variety of views you have about your activity, reflective writing can become an exciting journey in self-exploration. Something that Alan Watts expresses far better than I can:

> The point, therefore of these arts, is doing them rather than the
> accomplishments. But more than this the real joy of them lies in what turns up

unintentionally in the course of practice, just as the joy of travel is not nearly so much in getting where one wants to go as in the unsought surprises which occur on the journey.

Watts, 1957

Your initial focus for reflective writing may be the narrow confines of a requirement to achieve professional acknowledgement by a professional body such as CILIP. However, human beings are notoriously dynamic in the way they work with their intelligence, and this process could happily spill over to allow you to glean powerful insights and learning which you will generalize to enhance your wider life.

All you need to do is start writing, and the process can begin.

5

The curriculum vitae

What is a CV?

A curriculum vitae (CV) may be defined as the story of your life but it is also an important statement about how you view yourself and a place for the projection of that view to others. Most of us need to compile a CV at some stage in our career, usually to apply for a new job or for a promotion. There are many books and websites giving advice on the preparation of a CV for these purposes. Much of this advice is useful if you are compiling a CV for the first time. The general rule is that you need to compile a CV as soon as you leave education. You can store copies of your CV electronically. Regularly review your CV to ensure that it is up to date and be prepared to re-present it to match the particular purposes and audiences that arise. Keeping your CV up to date is especially important as it is much easier to record important events or changes in your career as they happen than try to recall them from memory months or years later! Even if you are asked to complete an application form and not send a CV, your CV, if up to date, should provide most of the information you need for filling out the form.

The CV in your Portfolio

Compiling your full CV is probably the best place to start when you are preparing your Portfolio. It gives you an opportunity to record and review your knowledge and skills and to identify the key learning moments in your career to date. The CV in your Portfolio is slightly different from one you would normally use for a job or promotion. You are not restricted in length and you can annotate the entries. However, a word of caution: assessors will not be happy with extra long CVs; generally it is a good rule for them to be of two to four A4 pages, the final length dependent on the range of your experience.

Compiling your CV
General

Determining the style, layout and order of your CV is a personal choice but there are certain guidelines it is sensible to follow. Be concise, be confident (but honest), use only relevant information, and always give information in reverse chronological order, that is, the most recent first, whether you are talking about your experience, education or activities. It is for you to decide the order of information in your CV but include sections covering personal information (such as address details); knowledge and skills; work experience; education and training; professional activities; and, where appropriate, research undertaken and any publications. Perhaps the most important thing to remember in compiling a CV for your Portfolio is to make it easy for the assessor to know who you are and what you have done. Organize the information in a logical format and present the information clearly and concisely.

In your Portfolio application you are required to submit a personal statement and this has a strict word limit; if you are concentrating on the last two to three years there may be key developmental activities from earlier in your life that you want to reflect on. You may annotate your CV to show these key learning outcomes or substantial achievements, for example taking part in a project or job outside information and library work which developed your skills. Be brief, but show how this contributed to your professional development. Don't just describe what you did; think about the impact on you, your colleagues and the service.

Introduction and personal profile

There should be a personal or introductory section which includes your name, address and contact details. There is some disagreement about also including a personal profile. This is a short paragraph – of two or three sentences – highlighting your special qualities and skills. Most of us find it difficult to write this section and some employers or educators have expressed wariness about its use. However, it can be like those first 30 seconds in an interview and create a good first impression in the mind of the other person.

To prepare a personal profile, jot down three or four key things about yourself, for example:

- I am good with people.
- I have excellent IT skills.
- I have a lot of experience in finding information for users.

Then ask someone else to tell you, in no more than three sentences, what they admire about you or your work. Using these together, write a paragraph about yourself. Think about yourself as a product that you are marketing, or imagine you are travelling in a lift with the director of your company and that you have 45 seconds to tell her about yourself.

It is probably best to write the introduction after you have compiled the rest of your CV, even if it will actually appear very early on. Don't make any claims in this profile for which there is little supporting evidence in the body of the CV; for example, don't talk about being dynamic if nothing in your CV shows you as being dynamic. Also, if you do decide to use a personal profile – as with the rest of your CV – update it regularly!

Key skills and qualities

For many job applications it is very useful to have a separate section which identifies your key skills and qualities. It can act as an extension of the personal profile, if you have included one, and be a very useful guide to the package which makes up the rest of your CV. It is also an area where you can cross-reference to your personal statement, development plan and other evidence.

Some people prefer not to have a separate area on their CV for details of their skills and qualities but rather to integrate statements on key skills with the appropriate section on education or work experience. The choice is yours; by including it as a separate section, near the beginning of your CV, you are showing an ability to reflect on yourself and your abilities.

It is best to start the key skills section by listing your skills and qualities in draft; think about your technical or professional skills, interpersonal skills, ability to work or lead a team, teaching skills, and any management skills, including relating to finance. For help with articulating your knowledge and skills, look at the CILIP PKSB (see Chapter 6) and at the required skills as outlined in your job description.

When you have compiled this first draft try to quantify it as much as possible. Don't just use bland statements, for example mentioning that you have good IT skills. What exactly does that mean? If you say you are an experienced team leader, give examples of how you have demonstrated team leadership. Whatever you identify here, remember to give evidence of it elsewhere in your CV.

Work experience

This section is also sometimes referred to as employment history. Start with the most recent post and summarize the key responsibilities of each role you have held. Always take care to show the level, scope and scale of the post. If you have decided to include a section on key skills and qualities, as mentioned previously, do not repeat the information you have provided there in this section. Concentrate on your experience and any particular achievements (for example, running a successful event or receiving an award).

If appropriate, you can include voluntary work and any relevant part-time work here. Try to select aspects of that work which have developed you as an information professional, for example, dealing with customers, designing a website or financial responsibilities.

Education, qualifications and training

In this section give the details concisely and, as for the section above, in reverse chronological order. Keep annotation to a minimum.

You may decide to separate the information into two sections, listing educational qualifications first and then any training you have undertaken. The decision is yours and depends on the amount of information you wish to include. If you have recently completed a degree, at undergraduate or Master's level, and have written a dissertation as part of that course, you should include some information about it if the topic was relevant to library and information work. If you are studying for a higher degree you should include details of the topic of your thesis.

Whether presented as a separate section or not, you should list all training undertaken, including in-house training and courses attended. Remember to give dates. If you are an experienced information professional, and find that this list is very long, you may consider summarizing the information in this section and including a full list as part of the evidence you submit. Do not provide commentary in this part of your CV – you should demonstrate the outcomes of this training and any other professional development elsewhere in your Portfolio.

Professional activities

The emphasis in this section is on activity; it is an opportunity for you to outline the contribution you make to the profession. Membership of appropriate professional associations is expected; this must include CILIP, of course, but many information professionals find it important to belong to other associations and institutions. Active participation should be detailed in this section. This can include details of local and national meetings and conferences attended, presentations given, committees involved in, websites edited, being a mentor and so on. If you have a great deal of information to include in this section, it may be a good idea to subdivide it rather than just give a list by date; for example, you could split it into the sections CILIP regional Member networks or special interest group responsibilities, conferences, presentations and so forth.

Publications

Give full bibliographic details of anything you have had published, including articles in newsletters or house journals. You can include conference papers or research projects in this section or list them in separate sections. If you are a less experienced information professional it would be a good idea to include a copy of any article in your evidence; for those Members who have a lot of experience a detailed list is required here, with a sample of or extracts from recent papers in the evidence.

Other information

If you think that you have other relevant information to include in your CV which has not been covered in the sections listed above, you can consider having an additional section entitled 'Other information'. Often when applying for jobs it is usual to list other interests and activities, as this gives a rounded view of the applicant. The information you include here should be relevant to your Portfolio, however, and not be just a list of hobbies and interests. Participatory activities only should be included, and, if possible, you should reflect on the impact that the activities have had on you.

Hints and tips

- Think about your skills and knowledge and make sure to bring these out in your CV.
- Store your CV electronically and keep it up to date.
- Divide your CV into meaningful sections.
- Always give information in reverse chronological order, latest first.
- Use a concise and clear style.
- Where appropriate, annotate your CV to show important learning or experience, but keep it short.
- Use your CV as a 'selling point' for your Portfolio; the assessors do not know you so your CV should tell them a lot about you and your career.

Conclusion

As with all elements in the Portfolio, producing a CV enables you to identify key moments in your career and professional development and will make easier the task of matching your application to the criteria of assessment. Taking time with the structure and style will be repaid, as a well presented and carefully thought-through CV will act as a clear guide to the sort of information professional you are and create a good impression in the minds of others.

··
CASE STUDY 5.1
Karen Newton: My CV for Certification
··

For the first 27 years of my career I managed to get along fine without a CV; it never bothered me, I never bothered it, and we got along fine in ignorance of one other. Then one day CILIP launched the Certification of Affiliated Members and one of the main components within the Portfolio for assessment was a CV – help!

OK, I thought, I can do this, after all, it is only a CV, it is nothing to be scared of, all I have to do is write down my career history in order of the most recent first, should be a doddle. The CV went something like this:

1978–2005 Library Assistant, Sunderland Public Libraries

That was it – one employer for 27 years; the rest of the CV was simply blank, obviously not a good showcase of my skills and experiences!

Developing my CV

Back to the drawing board, or, in my case, my husband. A few months previously his employer had relocated so far away that the commute was now six hours a day, so, after not too much thought, he opted for redundancy and, like me, realized he needed a CV. 'Job Linkage' was based next door to the library I was working in, so he arranged a meeting and together they drafted a professional CV for him. Not being one to reinvent the wheel – I pinched it! It was no use as it stood, of course, but I could 'borrow' the layout, the formatting and the overall look of it and adapt it for my situation.

Handy tips included:

- Put the most relevant information first.
- Only put your education above work experience if you are a recent graduate, or if your qualification really is the most relevant aspect of your CV.
- Always list work experience and education in reverse chronological order, starting with the most recent activity.

Writing it all down

So, time to start getting it all down on paper. I wrote down all the positions I have held within Sunderland Libraries, encompassing the last 27 years, along with a brief outline of duties, concentrating on those which highlighted the aspects I wanted to relate to within the Portfolio as a whole. I started with the most recent, which at the time was:

2004–2006 Assistant Manager, Hetton Library
- Organize and administer the running of a large branch library and oversee the running of two part-time branches.
- Lead a team of eight assistants.
- Liaise with other departments within the building under the banner of 'People First'.
- Supervize all financial and budget transactions.
- Manage a programme of further education courses, both accredited and vocational.
- Allocate staff timetabling and annual leave.
- Monitor and report on targets.

And ended with my first post at 16 years old, which was:

1978–1983 Library Assistant
- Issue and return of stock.

- Shelving and repair of stock.
- Day-to-day issue-desk duties.

I kept the early years of my career relatively basic. However, for the later parts of my career there was much more to include and make reference to within my Portfolio.

My education was along similar lines; one village school until I was 11, and then on to grammar school for O-levels – but once I had left school and started work, there was much more to add. In fact on my CV there is only one line on education, which says:

1973–1978 Houghton Grammar School, County Durham
- Seven O-levels

And that is the total of my pre-employment educational history, as it is just that – ancient history.

Training

More recent and, to my mind, much more relevant is the training and education I have undergone since I left school, from health and safety courses to communications workshops undertaken in-house, to a City & Guilds Library and Information Assistants Certificate taken by day release at the College of Arts and Technology, Newcastle. This could all be backed up by the evidence of certificates in my Portfolio, and these certificates came in very handy when I had to work out exactly when it was that I had attended the course.

Professional activities

When it came to writing down my professional activities and the publications that I had contributed to, there were more than I initially thought. I obviously enjoy working in a library, which came as a bit of a surprise! These were added to my CV as well – once again in reverse chronological order, with the most recent first. But don't think that by 'professional activities' I mean just working with CILIP; make sure that any project work you have helped with is included, such as refurbishments or reorganizations, major stock edits, promotional work, for example, the Summer Reading Challenge and so on. You should also list any relevant experience outside of work – for example, committee or unpaid work, treasurer for a parent–teacher association or volunteering as a Brownie pack leader. And also include staff newsletters and web pages.

Conclusion

My CV was finally completed. It was too long for a normal CV, but was not to be used for a job application; it was to be used to demonstrate my abilities and knowledge, and would, hopefully, go towards a successful ACLIP Portfolio. One of the main things to remember when compiling a CV in this case is that there is no size or word restriction. Usually a CV has a maximum of two pages; in this instance it can be longer to include a lot of additional information that may not fit into the size-restricted personal statement and development plan. You can cross-reference from your CV to the Portfolio contents, but I found that it did not work well for me; it looked more messy than informative.

So how have we got on together since then? Quite well thank you. We go out together to various events, and once I even sent it off all by itself for an actual job application. Oh and I have taken advice and keep it up to date with regular rewrites, so it always looks fresh and current – just like its owner on a good day.

CASE STUDY 5.2
Jim Jackson: The Certification experience

The CV can be used to document additional tasks which there might not be room for in other parts of the Portfolio. It is generally accepted that the CV needs to be in reverse chronological order of employment and qualifications, with your current post showing what position you hold. I found putting together a CV very challenging as I had not produced one for many years and wanted to expand on some of my experiences, the opportunities I had taken and, of course, my successes. This needed to be done not as an academic essay but as a brief and concise evaluation of all that I had learned. Of all the skills a library assistant learns, evaluation is the most important. Descriptive skills are, of course, important but an analysis of what you have done and what you have gained shows why you should be offered opportunities for CPD. My CV shows my progression from library assistant working in a small departmental library to senior information assistant and library supervisor for a branch library. There is a progression of training, application of new skills, forward planning and professional involvement in external events and organizations. Membership of the appropriate group of CILIP cannot be overestimated as it provides valuable opportunities to participate in and contribute to activities to which you may not have access at work.

All of this can be apparent from a clear and concise Portfolio, with a good CV at the front to invite the assessor to look carefully at the rest of the evidence in the Portfolio. Your CV reflects your past successes while your personal development plan shows your future plans and objectives. It is important to consider the Portfolio as an integrated set of items rather than separate documents, as it can demonstrate what a candidate has achieved, how they did it, what they learned from it all, and where they want it to take them. It is possible to use the CV to cross-reference to other evidence, but I found this very difficult to do. I also think it detracts from the important information that the CV is trying to convey.

CASE STUDY 5.3
Margaret Watson: My CV for Fellowship

When I finally committed myself to applying for Fellowship of CILIP I did wonder where I should start. I did have lots of 'stuff' – hard copies of documents and electronic files – and a vague idea of the themes I wanted to concentrate on. I had decided to make my application based on the contribution I believe I had made to library and information studies education, in particular in ensuring the integration of theory and practice, and on the contribution I had made to the profession. Being a very practical person I decided to start on the obvious, and what I thought might be the 'easiest' part of the Portfolio – revising my CV.

Because of the work involved in the revision of my CV and reflecting on my career to date, I found this a very useful 'kick start' to the whole business of making my application. I also quite enjoyed looking back at some of my earlier CVs and job applications. There were some things I had forgotten all about! I also became aware of a pattern which I perhaps would not have otherwise discovered: my career was not planned in a formal way, but clearly information literacy and dealing with users provided the basis of much of my work. This interest in helping users find the information they required eventually developed into teaching library and information studies. Reflecting on the way my career had developed, the choices I had made and the decision to be an active Member of my professional association was useful in preparing the whole application.

Back to the work on the CV! The university where I taught required all staff to keep an up-to-date CV in electronic form and in a very specific format. However, apart from qualifications, the university CV was only to cover the last five years. So when I looked at my current CV it was only a starting point. I had been a Chartered Librarian since 1967, so a great deal had happened in those intervening years. Fortunately I had kept e-copies of CVs I had used to apply for promotion within the university and I also had paper copies of earlier CVs from when I had applied for other jobs. So my first task was to assemble a master CV. This is my first piece of advice – don't do what I did – do as I say! Keep your CV up to date at all times and have a master CV which you can then use or adapt to meet the circumstances. I needed a much fuller CV than the one I was using and it was quite a task to get it organized properly.

Annotating the CV

One of the major problems of submitting my Fellowship so late in my career was that there was such a lot of information I could include. It was perfectly obvious that the word limit on the personal statement meant that I had to focus very clearly and not include information which was peripheral to the submission. I discussed the problem of trying to put a gallon into a pint pot with a friend, who just replied, 'Annotate the CV.' It was one of those lightbulb moments! This meant that I could highlight important elements in my career or personal development in the CV and not need to include them in the other parts of the Portfolio. The CV could then really be the story of my career, which would be part of the evidence I used to address the assessment criteria.

Two examples of this use of annotating my CV came from earlier posts:

1979-1987 Assistant Librarian, Humanities, Sunderland Polytechnic
I had responsibility for collection development, online information retrieval and user education in eight subject disciplines and achieved a high level of success in liaising with academic staff.

1968-1972 Assistant Librarian and Information Officer, University of Newcastle upon Tyne
I became the first Information Officer and was responsible for introducing the first user education programme across the university.

These statements provided a link between my earlier work and the focus in my personal statement on education and training of library and information professionals.

I also listed a wide variety of professional activity over the last 20 years and added the following notation:

* Professional activity over the last 16 years has informed my teaching and research and has enabled me to bring together practitioners and educators in our discipline.

This statement picked up points I was making in my personal statement and for which I had other supporting evidence.

Organizing the CV

I decided to organize my CV into seven sections:

• Personal information – name and status.

- Qualifications.
- Employment – this was the largest section and needed to be very clearly set out. My last post had two distinct elements: the work I did in the subject department as principal lecturer, and the work I did within the wider university. I briefly annotated the entries where appropriate.
- Professional activities – I included a couple of annotations here.
- Research and consultancy.
- Courses and conferences – I divided this section into two: courses and conferences I had organized or spoken at and those I had attended.
- Publications.

It is important to remember that the assessors who look at your application only see what you have presented to them. They do not know you so it is crucial that they can look at your CV and get a real feeling for you as an information professional. The CV is a very valuable part of your supporting evidence. As with everything in my application I asked my husband to read my CV. He is not a librarian so it was very useful to get an objective opinion.

Keeping the CV up to date

So what have I done with my CV since getting my Fellowship? As I am now retired, why should I bother? As I am still involved with training mentors and assessors I need to make sure that I keep my knowledge and skills up to date so that I have credibility in the profession. Through CILIP I have also become involved in new areas of work such as diversity and ethics, so am still learning. So I have compiled a 'master' CV without the annotations and try to keep that up to date. I have also set up a folder on my PC in which I can store any relevant documents, such as evaluations and course information. I have found the Revalidation audit sheet really useful to help me to reflect on professional activities, but have to admit that I don't use it as much as I should; I still keep a big box to store hard copy 'evidence'. So the verdict is 'Can still do better'!

6

The Professional Knowledge and Skills Base

What is the Professional Knowledge and Skills Base?

The Professional Knowledge and Skills Base (PKSB) encompasses the broad range of skills that are required by workers across all sectors of the library, knowledge and information profession. It is an interactive PDF which can be found at www.cilip.org.uk/cilip/jobs-and-careers/ professional-knowledge-and-skills-base and can be used as:

- a self-assessment tool for you to consider your personal and professional development needs and achievements
- a means of demonstrating your unique skills set to employers
- a framework for planning your CPD.

The PKSB is an essential part of professional registration and is a required document at all levels. It will assist you in demonstrating how you meet Criterion 1 of the CILIP assessment criteria (see Chapter 2 and Table 7.1) and may help you with the other criteria.

It consists of several elements:

- At the centre are ethics and values which underpin all work in the sector. All workers should have an understanding of these. A good starting point can be found at www.cilip.org.uk/cilip/about/ethics. Your employer may well have their own statement. A combination of both can provide useful food for thought which you could use to reflect on your views on the subject. Your reflections could form part of your evidence for criteria 2 and 3.

- Professional expertise and generic skills are broken down into sets of skills and knowledge which have been identified as essential to our profession. The 12 headings, shown on the wheel diagram, have in turn been broken down into further detail.
- All the above has been set within the wider library, information and knowledge sector context and the wider organization and environmental context. As required by Criterion 3 this shows the importance of maintaining current awareness and an understanding of the wider profession which exists outside your workplace.

How to use the PKSB

You are required to include two copies of your personalized PKSB in your application. The first should be completed as you start your application for professional registration; the second should be completed just before submitting your application. The interactive document, which you can only access if you are a Member of CILIP, enables you to record your self-assessment currently and at an ideal level. The comments box provides a space to give examples of how you can show that you have a particular skill or area of knowledge or how you intend to meet your ideal level.

If you wish to include retrospective CPD in your application for professional registration, you may want to complete your initial PKSB retrospectively too. This is perfectly acceptable.

Your level of knowledge and skills will vary from that of other people according to your organization, role, experience, sector and areas of interest. You may identify areas for development which are not relevant to your current role but which, because of your interest or ambitions, may help you in the future. It is up to you to decide what to include.

Remember that this document is intended for use across all sectors of the library, information and knowledge community. You are not expected to complete or even understand the whole document. Identify a few areas or sub sections which you wish to focus on and extract them from the document for inclusion in your Portfolio.

It can be helpful to discuss your ideas with your mentor or manager. They will help you to understand how your role fits into the areas identified in the PKSB. It is easy to ignore the obvious and the simple and to try to make everything too complicated. They will also be able to help you identify opportunities for filling the gaps that you have identified so that you can start putting together your plan. Ways of increasing your knowledge and skills may include reading, job shadowing, training in the workplace and elsewhere, attending events, talking to colleagues, visits and so on.

If when you work on your second version of the PKSB, in readiness for submitting your Portfolio, you have not completed everything you planned or hoped to cover, it does not matter. There may be all sorts of reasons for this, many of them beyond your control. You may also find that your activity log includes things which you did not include; this is equally acceptable.

The second version of the PKSB will form the basis of your evidence for Criterion 1.

Creating a development plan

Although you are not required to include a development plan in your Portfolio it can be very useful to do so. It should be a living document, which you update regularly and which does not stop when you achieve professional registration. It is also useful as a basis for Revalidation.

Any development plan is essential to the role we all have in the information business. Because the work is continually changing and our roles change fairly frequently it is important to be able to plan your continuing personal and professional development. Consider CPD as not something that just happens to you in an unstructured way, but rather as something in which you are pro-active, determining your goals and how you are going to reach them. CPD should be planned in such a way that your knowledge and skills are enhanced and improved by a programme of varied developmental activities. By formally recording your CPD you can track your development and think about the next steps: 'Personal planning provides direction, sets out objectives, identifies potential areas of development. It should not confine the individual; it must be flexible in order to accommodate unexpected opportunities and newly discovered skills and abilities; and must be regularly reviewed' (Webb and Grimwood-Jones, 2003). All through your career you will need to identify your developmental needs for the work you do, your future work, your employer and yourself.

Using the PKSB to carry out a skills and knowledge audit

Before you start any development plan carry out an audit of your skills and knowledge, as you need to know where you are starting from, where you want to go and how you will get there. This is where the PKSB comes in to play. But other documents can also help.

Sometimes the easiest place to start in your audit is to look closely at your job description. Check that you have the necessary skills and knowledge and record them. Consider any other duties you carry out in addition to the job specification; record the skills and knowledge that enable you to carry out those roles. Then think about other skills you have which are not, perhaps, part of your everyday work. Following all of this analysis, consider whether there are any gaps in your skills and knowledge that would enable you to do your job more effectively. It may just be updating your skills, or your job may recently have changed and you need to acquire a different skill set or more knowledge about a certain area of work.

Another way of starting is to carry out a SWOT (strengths, weaknesses, opportunities, threats) analysis; identify your strengths and weaknesses and any 'threats', which in CPD terms are the demands that you will be facing in the coming months. The 'opportunities' here will be the steps you can take to overcome those 'threats'. Consult one or two trusted colleagues and ask them to perform an informal SWOT analysis on you. Ask them to tell you three things you do well and three things you can improve on. If you have performance reviews or appraisal schemes at work you will be asked to identify training and development needs. Use the record of these meetings to help you with planning your development activities. As well as the advice from CILIP mentors and events run by CILIP, there are useful tools on the web to help you plan your personal development.

Setting goals

Once you know where you are starting from, think about setting goals. Most writers on this topic suggest using SMART goals. The goals you set yourself (or, in the case of an appraisal, are set for you, or in consultation with you) should be:

- specific
- measurable
- attainable
- relevant
- timed.

In other words, do not set yourself unrealistic and vague goals which you probably cannot achieve, will be difficult to measure and have no time limit on them. It is better to aim for five or six very clearly defined targets, which are achievable, normally within a year, rather than a wide-sweeping CPD plan. After all, the plan is dynamic and not set in stone. Life happens, work changes, and you may need to plot a different course.

Development activity

Having set your goals, then of course you must consider how you are going to achieve them. Remember that reaching your goal does not necessarily mean going on a course! You should use a wide range of activities to help in your development; these can include shadowing, attending meetings, chairing meetings, assisting in training, coaching other colleagues, reading, writing reports, project work and professional activities.

Reflecting on activity

Always record your developmental activity but also try to reflect on how well it has gone. What were the initial outcomes for you? What were the outcomes six months later? Did it meet your expectations? (See Chapter 4 for more ideas on reflective writing.)

Your comments can be very brief, just a few bullet points, but if you get into good habits early on in your career none of this recording and reflecting will seem difficult. Many organizations have good appraisal schemes where you have to reflect on the last 12 months and identify your development needs. Recording and reflecting on your development will help you both in your career and when you work towards professional registration.

The CILIP Portfolio section of the VLE provides a CPD activity log. Use this to record what you have done with your brief reflections on level of success or your learning outcomes. It will be a valuable piece of evidence in your Portfolio. Particularly for Chartership and Fellowship you could then select two or three activities from the log to reflect on in more detail and show how you have put your learning into practice, thinking about process and outcomes.

Certification

Your development plan is about forward thinking. When you are submitting your Portfolio you need to identify what you are going to do next. Your ACLIP application is about reflecting on your achievements to date and your development plan is looking ahead to maintaining and enhancing your skills and knowledge. You can also include activities which you are currently undertaking. For example, you may need to know more about reading development or helping customers to use online journals. One of the targets you might include would be moving on to Chartership after you have gained your ACLIP! If you do decide to go on to Chartership then your PKSB and any plan you draw up to achieve your targets should prove a very valuable tool.

Hints and tips

- Discuss your PKSB with your mentor or line manager.
- Write down what you are good at in your job.
- Identify what you can do to improve your skills and knowledge.
- Think about the next 12 months at work – are there any new developments in the service you will need to know about or any new areas of work you will have to undertake?
- Set yourself four or five realistic targets with a stated time for completion.
- Think about how you will know that the targets and your learning outcomes have been met.
- Keep a CPD activity log.
- Join the ACLIP discussion list.

Chartership

Putting together a Chartership Development Plan is not rocket science! Based on your personalized PKSB, it is intended to record where you are at the beginning of your professional registration process, where you need to get to, and the actions you intend to take in order to get there. It does not have to be complicated. Your PKSB and draft plan may form the basis of the first meeting you have with your mentor. Together you can discuss the various activities you will need to undertake. The initial version and the final version of your PKSB and its plan will not be the same because your development plan will change over the period of preparing your application. Your development is dynamic and reflects your personal growth over the whole period. You and your mentor will return several times to check on progress and make changes as appropriate to you and your work.

Applying for Chartership is not about being able to do everything and knowing all that there is to know about information work – it is about showing your ability to develop from your first qualification and a commitment to improvement and enhancement.

If you are submitting an application for Chartership when you have already been working for some years you may need to rethink your development plan slightly. Your mentor will advise you on this. Briefly, you will need to ensure that there is evidence of recent activity, but you may wish also to include some earlier CPD which has contributed to your growth as an information professional.

Hints and tips

- Prepare a PKSB and a draft plan and discuss it with your mentor.
- Set SMART goals.
- Be prepared to adapt your plan as circumstances change.
- Join the Chartership discussion list.
- Evaluate and reflect on all training and development activities.
- Review your progress regularly with your mentor and/or your manager.
- Update your plan regularly.
- Keep a CPD activity log.

Fellowship

Candidates for Fellowship should also use the PKSB as described above. However, as many Fellowship Portfolios will include evidence gathered over a long period of time, it is a good idea to be very selective in deciding what to include in a development plan. Fellowship candidates are expected to demonstrate a commitment to CPD throughout their career by using a CPD activity log and to show that that commitment is current.

Revalidation

When you start on the process of Revalidation it is a good idea to carry out a skills audit using the PKSB if you have not already done so for work. You can then plan your CPD based on that audit and complete the CPD activity log provided on the CILIP VLE.

I suggest that you use your PKSB and CPD activity log as the tool to help you identify your learning outcomes and evaluate all your training and development activity. This completed log forms the basis of your submission for Revalidation.

Hints and tips

- Use the CPD activity log to help you evaluate your CPD activity.
- Update your CPD log regularly.
- Update and review your audit sheet regularly.
- Use the CILIP Portfolio guidance on recording your CPD activities.

7

Evaluative statements

What is an evaluative statement?

In many ways the evaluative statement is the most important element in your Portfolio. Think of it as being rather like an executive summary in a report. If the report is long you should be able to get a very good idea of its contents from the summary. The executive summary almost stands as a document by itself. People should be able to read your evaluative statement and understand immediately what you are presenting about yourself and your development.

It may help you to think of the evaluative statement as a summary of the submission as a whole. If the evidence is a map of your development and achievements, then the evaluative statement is the key to understanding it.

The evaluative statement needs to show how you have met each of the assessment criteria and should link to the evidence that you have selected to demonstrate this. It is therefore helpful to have selected your supporting evidence first so that you can write an informative and reflective statement. It can be helpful to use the assessment criteria as headings in your statement (they are not included in the word count). This ensures that you cover all the assessment criteria and makes it easier to avoid becoming descriptive.

The evaluative statement is the one piece of reflective writing that *must* be in your Portfolio, although there should be other examples in the supporting evidence too. Your evaluative statement should show evidence of analysis, evaluation and review of your knowledge and experience.

Making a start

You will probably need at least two or three drafts before you are satisfied with your evaluative statement. The first draft I prepared for my Fellowship application was no good at all; it was really just a narrative version of my CV. However, writing it like that got it out of my system and helped me to concentrate on what I really wanted to say. Ultimately, I found it very useful to build my statement around the assessment criteria.

You will find it useful to discuss the early drafts of your evaluative statement with your mentor or a colleague, as they may have a more objective view. As a mentor I have found that most people are reluctant to 'boast' of their success and accomplishments. The length of the evaluative statement must not be more than 1000 words (not including headings), so you may wish to ask your mentor to assist with editing the statement to remove surplus information.

Always remember that the assessor will not know you and will not be familiar with your organization, so you have to make the evaluative statement purposeful and focused. But also beware – do not make any statements that are not substantiated by what is contained in the rest of the Portfolio. The easiest way to do this is to cross-reference the points you are making.

Writing your evaluative statement

By the time you write your evaluative statement you will have amassed a great deal of evidence. You will have gained a lot of work experience, perhaps attended conferences, courses, meetings or in-house training; you may have been involved in a project, visited other information services, participated in professional activities, and in many other developmental activities. Show how any evidence you are submitting meets the assessment criteria. A relatively easy way to map out your evidence and to ensure that you meet the criteria is to use a matrix as shown in Table 7.1.

The criteria form one axis and the developmental activities the other. You can then cross-reference all your evidence and all your developmental activities to the criteria. Remember that not all activities will meet all of the criteria – that is fine, so long as you have a good balance overall. When you look at the completed matrix you should be able to see the pattern of your evaluative statement emerge. You can then divide your evaluative statement into sections covering an introduction and the three criteria, and can show how your supporting evidence demonstrates that you meet all of the criteria. By doing it this

Table 7.1 How evidence submitted meets assessment criteria

Activity	Criterion 1	Criterion 2	Criterion 3	Evidence
	Identified areas for improvement in personal performance, undertaken activities, applied skills in practice, reflected on process and outcomes	Examined the organizational context of service, shown ability to implement or recommend improvement, reflected on actual or desired outcomes	Enhanced knowledge of wider professional context, reflected on areas of current interest	
Attended regional Members' Day	Partly – session on marketing relevant to skills gap identified in PKSB; need to plan practical application	Yes – opportunity to use exercise to apply content of presentation to my organization and discuss with other participants	Yes – networking with colleagues from other sectors; President's address highlighted current issues	Report to team (3.1) Article for branch newsletter (3.2) Plan for promoting new information service (2.3)
Participated in team meeting to develop service objectives	Yes – contributed ideas which were used, increased my confidence to express my views	Useful presentation of organizational aims from manager; helped me to understand our targets, to think about what we could improve, how I can contribute	Partly – can see how our budget situation reflects national situation which I have read about in *Update*	Aims statement with my annotations (1.4) My reflections after meeting (2.2) Notes of discussion with mentor about budget cuts (3.5)

way you can avoid simply describing what you have done.

The example shown uses the Chartership criteria but you can use the same matrix and substitute Certification or Fellowship criteria.

This is only a suggestion – don't forget that the Portfolio belongs to you and is a personal and unique account of your professional development. You can get lots of advice from your mentor and local candidate support officer, and you should find the time to attend at least one professional registration event.

Many candidates worry that 1000 words is not enough to include everything that they want to say. Your evaluative statement is an overview and summary. It is perfectly acceptable to write evaluative reports or commentary as part of you evidence. You can then focus on one particular aspect of your learning or the organization's objectives or an event and make your personal evaluation in a focused and concise way.

Each evaluative statement is unique and the claims that each of us make are very different. However, the common factor is the need to reflect and focus on the key areas. Look at the assessment criteria, look at the evidence that you have collected, select a few pieces of evidence which have the strongest links to the criteria and build your statement around them. I have found it very interesting to work with colleagues who are thinking about applying for professional registration at all three levels and to get them to focus on their achievements.

You know you are evaluating if you:

- are not describing what has happened
- have measured and given your personal views on effectiveness
- can demonstrate that you have put your learning into practice
- are asking and answering questions
- have said what has changed and what has been done as result.

Hints and tips

- Decide on the key points you want to make in your evaluative statement.
- Keep it clear and concise – remember the 1000 word limit.

- Do not just describe what you have done – evaluate and review your development. Use the 'so what?' principle.
- Cross-reference to other elements in your Portfolio.
- Look at examples of statements on the CILIP website.
- Discuss drafts with your mentor or a critical friend.
- Go to professional registration event.
- Remind yourself of the assessment criteria.

CASE STUDY 7.1
Calderdale Libraries: Sarah Cockroft, Roberta Crossley and Heather Karpicki: The personal statement for Certification

Five librarians from Calderdale Libraries worked together on their ACLIP applications. They all had a great deal of prior experience in libraries or related work.

Writing the personal statement

Having worked for Calderdale Libraries for a considerable number of years we felt that we ought to do something to cement our knowledge and experience.

It was really important to focus on what we had achieved, what we can achieve and what we hope to achieve. We had to find out how to reflect on what we had learned from our various working experiences. It was not easy at first to do this as we were initially far too descriptive, something which is perhaps natural when you want to make clear how tasks were achieved to someone who does not know what you have done. It is not sufficient, however, to say 'I achieved this and this is how I did it'; we had to think about how it changed us and made us more confident in accepting new challenges. We also had to show how we approached things differently when dealing with similar situations, thus showing how we had grown and matured. Throughout this we gained an overview of how we have each developed and how our past experiences have paved the way for the roles we now fulfil.

Matching the assessment criteria

A valuable time was when we all met our mentors to share the things we had done as this prompted us to remember additional things we had forgotten about. The difficulty was matching the evidence with the assessment criteria, as it appeared that some of the criteria could overlap, but that was fine. The important thing was to choose examples of work experience and then be concise in stating what we had learned and how we grew in confidence.

We needed evidence to go with our statements so it was important to choose carefully the examples we were giving. In many ways, once you have started the process of reflection the difficulty in completing is not what to include, but rather what to leave out, and how to edit down all the information you have. It makes you realize just how varied your job is and how wide your skill set has developed as a result.

It is worthwhile getting into the habit of writing evaluations of events, workshops or training as well as any particular problems you have dealt with. Save any correspondence that might be useful to support what you are stating has happened, such as what a colleague may have sent you in support of some work project you have undertaken, particularly anything praising and acknowledging your input.

The mentors

The mentors gave valuable advice and offered constructive criticism of where we needed to change things. The key things we learned we had to remember are:

- Keep the statement brief and be concise and not too descriptive – remember it is about you and how you reacted and what you learned.
- Get into a reflective mentality, always questioning, 'What did I learn?', 'How have I grown?', 'What do I do different now?'
- Cross-reference at every opportunity to make sure you mention all the evidence you have used.
- Save anything that might be useful – e-mails, newspaper cuttings, programmes of events you have organized, thank-you notes,

photographs, examples of anything you have done to help improve the service, be that creating a simple form or putting workshop material together.

- Remember to de-personalize any examples you put in your Portfolio.
- Don't overload your Portfolio with evidence but make the evidence you have work for you. You can use a good piece of evidence to cover a couple of statements.
- Stick to the assessment criteria.
- Be professional when putting your Portfolio together – no scruffy handwritten labels.
- Think carefully about the layout of your Portfolio and try to put it together always thinking that someone will be reading it who does not know who you are or the full nature of your job.
- Set out the evidence references against your statements clearly.
- Use your mentor.

Moving on

The personal statement also helps to identify the areas of development and training you still require in order to move into new work experiences. A valuable lesson learned was that we gained an overview of our strengths and likely future development. We also understood more about seeing the 'bigger picture' of how our work fits in with the service as a whole, and gained a more rounded view of ourselves as people.

CASE STUDY 7.2
Paul Tovell: Writing the evaluative statement for my Chartership Portfolio

I never wanted my Chartership assessors to read my diary. But that notebook carefully hidden many years ago was the last time I had dabbled in reflective writing. If only I had kept it up, I found myself thinking after my Chartership workshop, the evaluative statement of my Portfolio would be easy. Instead, the prospect of 'reflecting' was now a daunting one. Not only did I feel alarmed at the thought of submitting something so personal, but also there were so many ways it could go wrong. Reflective writing can be repetitive and irrelevant, and the word limit left no room for waffle. This was my big chance to demonstrate professional competence – it was definitely not the place for vague sentiments like 'I enjoyed my day out because it was nice.'

Apprehensively, I contacted my mentor. But when we discussed it, I realized that I did not have to write a diary entry, nor a literary masterpiece with a plot and a dastardly villain. I only needed to write a glorified index. The sole job of this paragraphed contents list was to explain briefly why every document was included. If it did that, it would succeed as an evaluative statement, be suitably reflective, and tie together my whole Portfolio. And all in just 1000 words!

I had come to libraries in a very traditional way: a first degree, then a trainee year, followed by a Master's in Librarianship. At the start of the traineeship, I went to a formal talk with a lecturer from the nearby library school, and he was the first to hammer home the importance of Chartering as soon as possible – for the money, the career prospects and the contacts. I still remember my initial horror at the thought of yet more hurdles. But there was so much help at hand – and he was right. When I started work, I found that my library authority was very keen on putting all new recruits straight onto a training programme in order to see the wider professional context. This created a strong, supportive network which transferred very naturally into a Chartership support network. The obligatory workshop and mentor were arranged for us with no hassle, and all we then needed to do was prepare the Portfolio. The bottom drawer of my desk became a deposit box and the documents, many more than I would ever use, piled up.

Collating the evidence

By the time the drawer was overflowing, I needed a little guidance to help with the collating. CILIP's three assessment criteria, once I had thought about what they really meant, gave me the signposting I needed. But before I matched my documents to them, I needed to convince myself of the reasons that every particular piece of work was included. One of them demonstrated my teamwork skills, which have greatly improved since I started work.

Another showed how I had applied my new knowledge to a specific problem which needed solving. If I could not persuade myself (and you know who they say is your harshest critic), then the document was rejected. If I could persuade myself, then the reason went into the evaluative statement.

I quickly realized that I would soon end up with a jumbled mess unless I gave the statement a tight structure. Having virtually memorized the assessment criteria by this point, I used them to outline clear and direct paragraphs. No introduction or conclusion, just the meat of the evidence. Now I had a framework I could use, along with those key sentences and phrases to slot in. The first word count was rather excessive, and it took some editing to remove repetitions and to shorten sentences to their snappiest and sharpest format. My mentor's proofreading was invaluable: someone else can often spot what your own eyes skim past. By the time I had pared it down to 1000 words, I definitely had an evaluative statement and not, to my relief, a diary.

Selecting the evidence

Cross-referencing (putting numbers in brackets all over the place) should be easy. At least, if the documents stay where they are, it should. In reshuffling, removing and replacing documents I ended up renumbering them at least three times. Nonetheless, the process was a foolproof way of ensuring that I referred to every piece of evidence in the evaluative statement. As I struggled to include more than 25 items of evidence in the 1000 words, this actually made the statement an easy way of limiting the number of documents to include in the Portfolio.

I had to make some tough decisions. My involvement in a local studies publication was surprisingly hard to tailor to meet the criteria. Without matching the criteria, it would have actually weakened the Portfolio. Later I noticed that I was using two sets of meeting minutes, and I had selected them both for the same reason. Duplication is pointless, and one set had to go. It was not until I wrote the evaluative statement that these glitches really stood out. But, consequently, in the finished Portfolio no page was wasted, and I had ensured that every document had really earned its right to be there.

Conclusion: giving shape to your career

Since I hit the ground running, having known about Chartership before I started work, I was able to complete my Portfolio in a year. The process itself really focused my attention on my career and personal development. When I started job-hunting in the middle of it all, I found I had valuable information ready to hand: development needs and examples of good work are both prime interview material. Preparing for Chartership also stimulates a supportive network of people in the same position as yourself, either physically in your local area or virtually via discussion lists. These contacts may last for your entire career. It is hard to appreciate the journey when you feel overburdened and pressured. But it is worth it, and it is not just jumping through hoops. You are putting your career into shape by creating a Portfolio. You will hone your strengths and address your weaknesses by doing some reflective writing. And you may as well use all those skills you developed when you last wrote in a diary.

CASE STUDY 7.3
Sue Westcott: Writing the evaluative statement for my Fellowship Portfolio

What is Fellowship?

What does the word 'Fellowship' conjure up in your mind? For me, as a childhood devotee of all things Tolkien, it meant a band of friends, with different strengths, weaknesses and personalities, hopes and dreams, on a long journey with a clear end in mind. There are difficulties to overcome, challenges to enjoy, and dragons and demons to be avoided, all made easier by the strength of your relationship with fellow travellers. My career has very much been like that and achievement of my Fellowship was no different. What my Fellowship also gave me was a wonderful way to reflect, be clear about my role and decide how I wanted that journey to continue.

So, Fellowship, surely that is for 'Fellows'? For the great and the good? For those with national careers or experience based on academic excellence? Not for someone who still felt at the end of the first phase of her career who, although she had achieved a certain amount, felt that that had been through working with her colleagues, through doing her job and who certainly did not have the wealth of experience and achievements of some of her peers? Surely, if I applied for Fellowship I would be found out. . . . Well, I am living proof that that is not true – Fellowship is not the preserve of those rare, exalted few, looking towards a well deserved retirement. It is something we should all consider when we have sufficient experience and achievement to demonstrate our professional experience since Chartership.

Why Fellowship?

How did my journey begin? I was very fortunate in that my first post was in a government library which had a clear programme to work towards Chartership, and that my chief librarian was very supportive throughout that process and then insisted that I got on and submitted my Chartership, achieving it within two years of starting my first professional post. I remember the thrill of knowing that my professional body recognized my abilities. Years passed, I changed posts, learned new skills and got involved in CILIP (The Library Association as it was then) through my specialist interest group and then went on to be the councillor for the group. All with good friends and colleagues supporting and encouraging me. A series of career development workshops made me realize that although I had clearly made considerable progress in my career I had no yardstick to measure this by and, being a rather goal-orientated individual, I began to look for a yardstick. Occasionally, someone would suggest Fellowship, but it would pass me idly by, on my mental 'to do' list, when I had time, when there were not other things to do. Increasingly, however, it came up in conversation with three particular friends, and together we resolved to do something about it.

Preparing the statement: team work

Having committed, we were then faced with the prospect of actually applying, but having all promised each other, no one could back out. We were all equally busy, all equally unsure where to start, and all trying to work out why we thought we should be Fellows. First we checked what we had to do by obtaining the CILIP guidance and making sure we all understood it. We got examples of key documents from CILIP's very helpful Qualifications and Professional Development Department. We began to identify the evidence we wanted to base our applications on – much hunting around in old computer files, boxes of career documents, lofts, drawers at work and so on. We each drafted a CV and circulated it to one another and commented – identifying areas where someone had not expressed their achievements clearly enough, or where perhaps more detail was needed – as we knew that assessors who did not know us, our work, or the sectors we had worked in would be making the decision on our application.

The most intimidating requirement was the statement setting out why each of us thought we were worthy of CILIP's highest achievement. To support each other, we set one Saturday aside and spent the day at Maggie's. Each with our own space to work and no distractions we had no choice but to get on and put finger to laptop. Periodically we would re-group, be rewarded with cake and coffee, lunch, wine and nibbles, and would critically examine each other's documents and make suggestions for improvement in structure and content, and remind each other of the achievements we had gained (and sometimes forgotten).

How on earth to start? That first sentence took me more effort than the rest of the statement put together. We all took different approaches but, generally speaking, we each identified two or three themes, which would tie our evidence together and fitted the criteria for Fellowship. In my case the focus was on knowledge and development of the government library sector, professional involvement in CILIP, and work in the wider information management environment. The day passed into the evening and by dinner we had each got a CV and a statement, which only needed finer tuning. All of us pulled together our Portfolios and off they went to CILIP shortly afterwards. The result was four very proud individuals at Members' Day in November.

Conclusion

Three years on, what has it all meant? The process of writing my applications made me reflect on what I have enjoyed most and what I have got most satisfaction from in my career. I have used that to develop a very loose plan for moving forward and now have a new job, on the fringes of information management, where there is plenty of opportunity to try new things and learn new skills. I have spoken about Fellowship with enthusiasm to other colleagues who had achieved a lot but felt unworthy, several of whom as a result have gone on to achieve Fellowships too. It has also got me into better habits. I now keep my CV up to date, and keep a better archive and a list of achievements and professional development. I have always been an advocate of Revalidation, and so in the next year I will measure once again how far I have come professionally.

8

Supporting evidence

What is supporting evidence?

The supporting evidence is probably the largest part of your Portfolio. You will have collected a great deal of evidence of your professional developmental activities over the last year or two. The most important things to remember are that each piece of evidence should demonstrate that you meet the criteria for the relevant level, each document should support the points made in your evaluative statement, and you can evidence a variety of developmental activities over a period of time.

Selecting your evidence

You will probably not need to include all the evidence you have collected; choose your evidence well. If you have used a matrix to record your developmental activities against the assessment criteria, as suggested earlier, you should find the whole process of choosing and sorting your evidence easier. Later in this chapter Ruth Wilkinson gives an example of how the matrix can be used in Chartership. The matrix should also help you to identify any gaps in your evidence. The aim is to choose items for your Portfolio which are core to your application. There may be some of your documents which repeat the same point as others and can thus be omitted; for example, you don't need to include copies of all your PowerPoint presentations or all the information leaflets you have created. A sample of presentations, talks or flyers is sufficient. As Isabel Hood (2006) says, 'Portfolios become slimmer with experience in constructing them and length of professional practice.'

One of the most frequently asked questions at CILIP professional registration events is how much supporting material should be included? The answer, predictably, is 'As much as is necessary to show how you meet the assessment criteria'! For Certification you do not really need more than ten pieces of evidence. So be selective. There may be more supporting evidence for Chartership and Fellowship candidates but, again, quality is more important than quantity. My strong advice here is to seek individual guidance from your mentor or the candidate support officers in your area.

Types of evidence

So what kind of evidence can you use? The answer is anything that shows your professional development. There is no prescriptive list. All of us have very different stories to tell of our development and will choose the most appropriate documents to support that story. Common items include:

- evaluations of conferences and training
- service aims and objectives with notes to show how you contribute to them and/or your views on how successfully they are met
- information you have created for users
- extracts from reports
- extracts from published articles
- extracts and notes from presentations
- performance reviews or appraisal records
- minutes of meetings
- visit reports
- web pages
- blogs
- annotated bibliographies
- training plans.

If you are a Chartership candidate choose materials that show that you understand the objectives of the organization you work for, and of the information services and products that the organization provides. But, very importantly, you also need to evaluate how those objectives are being met. This is a very good opportunity to include a piece of reflective writing. Don't just give the results of any surveys carried out; try to draw your own conclusions and suggest ways to improve the service.

Make your evidence relevant

You need to upload your evidence to your VLE account as you go along. Make sure that the evidence is appropriate and shows that you meet the assessment criteria. The assessor needs to be able to understand what the evidence means. So, for example, only include organizational structure charts if they show where you fit in; only include minutes of meetings if they show your contributions; if including a report or article produced by a team, make sure it is clear how exactly you contributed to it; and don't send copies of every certificate you have if all they show is that you attended a course! You can annotate any documents you include if explaining their relevance a little more would be beneficial; it is an opportunity to show your evaluation and reflective skills. So, as you add your pieces of evidence to your file, write a note about the evidence to make it easier when you come to collate all the material and reflect further.

Reflect on your evidence

If you start in a methodical way at the beginning of the process, you can also get into good habits of reflection. Before you upload your evidence, think about it and make some notes for yourself. For example, if it is a certificate of training, evaluate the training, and comment on how you plan to apply the new skills acquired and knowledge learned; this will be useful when you come to review the evidence and write your evaluative statement. It is much easier to make a note immediately after an event than try to remember what happened some time later, when it is no longer fresh in your mind. If you have visited another information service, record your opinions of that service and make a note of anything you could use in your workplace. If you are required to write a report on any conference or presentation you attend, keep a copy of it – if not required for work, try doing it for yourself! If you have given a presentation or led a training event, make sure you evaluate it and write up what went well and what could have been better. Become a reflective practitioner. It may seem strange at first, making notes for yourself about what you do at work, but gradually it will become second nature.

If you are an experienced practitioner you may already have a great deal of evidence which you will need to sort through and arrange into some form of logical sequence. This is probably more difficult than starting off in an organized way. You may, like me, discover that some of the evidence has disappeared into the ether. If you are applying for Certification, Chartership or Fellowship after more than five years, concentrate on the last two to three, although, for Fellowship, evidence of achievement throughout your whole career is important. Use your annotated CV to evidence your professional development before the period you are concentrating on. You can include lists of courses and conferences attended and can annotate those lists with some reflective comments. Then, using the appropriate matrix, try to map your developmental activities and the evidence against the criteria.

As a mentor one of the most useful things I have found is to ask my mentees to produce a contents list of the evidence they are going to submit. This makes you think about the choice of evidence and its organization. Producing the contents list for another person ensures that the structure makes sense to someone else. Often we are too close to our own Portfolio to review its structure critically.

Information about the evidence required to show that you have worked with a mentor is discussed in Chapter 3.

Evidence for Revalidation

The approach to presenting the evidence for Revalidation is by using the ongoing CPD log in your CPD area of the CILIP Portfolio. Use this to help you reflect on the learning outcomes of your training and development.

Letters of support for Fellowship applications

Letters of support are a required element of the Portfolio for Fellowship only. There should be at least two and they should be from people who can best endorse your suitability. One letter must be from your mentor. Once you have decided whom to ask, you should ask them as promptly as possible, make sure they understand what is required and let them have a copy of the guidelines and the assessment criteria. Always give them a deadline, and if you do not hear from them, do get back in touch.

How many letters of support you decide to include will very much depend on the application you are making. For some Fellowship applicants, much of the evidence will be in published books and articles; for others letters of support from senior colleagues will be important. When I applied for my Fellowship I felt that I should seek support from people with whom I had worked within my organization and regionally. They endorsed the evidence that I provided and gave an added perspective to my evaluative statement.

Organizing your evidence

Once you have decided on what evidence you are going to include you should decide how you will organize it so that the assessor can easily look from the evaluative statement to the appropriate evidence. Always remember that you know how everything fits together, but that you are presenting the Portfolio to other Chartered Members who do not know you or where you work. Make it easy for the assessors to find the information they need through cross-referencing or direct links.

Hints and tips

- Start collecting your evidence as soon as you can.
- Annotate the evidence where appropriate.
- Organize evidence into broad categories.
- Use a matrix to map evidence against criteria.
- Review and revise your evidence file regularly so you can ensure you have all the evidence you need.
- Select specific evidence needed to meet the assessment criteria.
- Compile a contents list.
- Avoid repetition and duplication.
- Remember quality not quantity.

CASE STUDY 8.1

Ruth Wilkinson: Supporting evidence for my Chartership Portfolio

On commencing my role as information specialist at National Building Specification (NBS) I became a Member of CILIP and went along to a Chartership workshop. We carried out a series of exercises that helped me to reflect on the value and purpose of training. I used the results of these exercises to assess where I needed further training and discussed this with my manager at my next performance review.

A fairly new graduate, I needed to complete the year of professional experience before applying. During this year my training objectives were to gain more construction-industry-orientated knowledge to enable me to understand the information needs of my client group. I also needed to refresh my information skills and become more proficient at using Microsoft Access. This was achieved by attending a number of courses, visits and knowledge-sharing seminars, professional reading, a conference and activities within my team.

Building evidence

In some cases I was asked to take notes and distribute them for the benefit of the rest of the information services team. This was useful evidence to support event handouts and certificates of attendance; I began to organize a folder containing material from each event I had attended. I also wrote a personal reflection after each event, which highlighted the value of the training and its relevance to my personal and professional development.

I registered under the new Chartership regulations in May 2006, along with three other members of my team. It made sense for us all to try to get the same mentor and help each other through the process. The first meeting with our mentor was to discuss the personal and professional development plan and material for evidence. We had prepared a list of questions, and after the meeting my understanding was that many types of evidence could be used so long as they met the criteria of assessment. I also planned to use evidence obtained prior to registration, as it was relevant to my development. Our mentor suggested that we use a table containing the criteria of assessment as headings, and then enter our activities to see how they met the criteria. She called this a Chartership matrix (Table 7.1). I found this a very worthwhile exercise, as it defined the importance of the training and displayed patterns of development.

Reviewing professional evidence

I spent the next month working on my CV and personal professional development plan (now PKSB audit). My training requirements are discussed every six months at performance reviews and, although training was driven by work activities, my employer encouraged me to attend events that would broaden my knowledge within the library profession. The records of my performance reviews provided a good framework for the personal professional development plan. I also tried to include as much information as possible on my CV; I cross-referenced to it from my personal statement. This was a good way of keeping the word count down and providing a clear picture of skills gained and achievements to date.

I chose to revisit the notes from the Chartership workshop to try to define the skills I needed to develop through training. I carried out a SWOT analysis and gave it to three people who knew me well to make comments. I also carried out a skills audit (Figure 8.1), using skills mentioned in the CILIP Body of Professional Knowledge (PKSB). I found both of these exercises interesting; they illustrated my strengths and weaknesses, which helped me set objectives for my personal professional development plan and performance reviews.

When completing the Chartership matrix I returned to my original notes from courses attended. In some cases I had found the course interesting but not that useful. As time passed my views changed and I was able to apply some of the skills or knowledge gained to my work activities. This has taught me to be more open minded about training opportunities and to try to enhance my knowledge of the profession outside my work activities.

Drafting my statements

I agreed with my mentor to try to get a draft personal and evaluative statement written by the end of August. This proved difficult to begin with, so I used the Chartership matrix (Table 7.1) and personal professional development plan to identify areas of development and material to support it. I received feedback on my statement and was then asked to provide a draft contents page. I felt this exercise really clarified what evidence to include and gave me a framework of what my Portfolio would contain. I decided to split the evidence into five sections: organizational context, personal performance, service performance, commitment to CPD and professional knowledge.

Using the draft contents page I began to build a rough Portfolio. This highlighted areas where I needed to provide more evidence and amend my personal statement. I had another meeting with my mentor in October, when we went through my draft Portfolio. In essence she was satisfied that I was on the right track and that I just needed to write it all up. We agreed that I would try to submit before the end of 2006. During this time I continued to attend events and participate in activities that would contribute to the Portfolio. I began to take charge of my personal and professional development.

Finally, I submitted my Portfolio in January 2007. I was lucky to have the support of a good mentor and work colleagues; I also joined an informal Chartership group in my area which met every few months and had an e-mail forum. Once I was clear what was required, I enjoyed putting the Portfolio together and I feel it has given me a sense of achievement and a vision for the future.

Subject knowledge   **Information dissemination**
    Document processing   **Indexing**
    Communication
Understanding user information need   Document construction
    Metadata   **Content analysis**   Abstracting
Content evaluation   **Secondary processing**   **Document selection**
    Document storage   Cataloguing   **Classification**
Document preservation   Records management Data mining
    Information retrieval   Website and portal design
Database maintenance   **Information service moderation**
Information service analysis Information ethics   **Customer service**
User behaviour   Information regulations   **Intellectual property**
    Accessibility   **Computer literacy**   **Interpersonal skills**
Management skills   Marketing   Training   Mentoring   **Research**

Note
I have gained some skills in abstracting and records management but feel that there is still room for improvement in these areas. This exercise was very useful prior to my annual performance review where I have the opportunity to request training needs and ensure that development is in areas where I am weak.

Figure 8.1 Skills Audit – 1 August 2006 (based on Career Development Group worksheet)

The skills shown in Figure 8.1 have been taken from the CILIP Body of Professional Knowledge. Those in bold indicate competent skills gained from my career at NBS to date.

CASE STUDY 8.2
Ayub Khan: Supporting evidence for my Fellowship Portfolio

My evidence categories

The type of documentary or other evidence you present can be any material you believe relevant to your personal statement. I included the following:

- research that I undertook on particular projects during my career, including work on a new library project I was working on at the time
- published material – sample copies of articles I had published in the professional literature and PowerPoint presentations I had given
- evidence of practical professional achievement of any kind such as my National Vocational Qualification (NVQ) assessor's Certification, awards, reports and papers I was particularly proud of

- accounts of professional work with supporting evidence, including committee meeting minutes, strategies and policy papers I had produced and conferences that I had organized or attended.

I tried to include projects that I had worked on in my current job or within the last few years for currency, although for some evidence I drew on a longer period.

Evaluating your evidence

Remember that it is important to be evaluative but not descriptive. For example, I attended Umbrella, so said, 'I attended the Umbrella conference in Hatfield and found it really useful to attend the seminars and meet colleagues from other sectors. I learned the frustrations that staff are experiencing in the HE sector, concerning access to electronic resources. I realize that public library staff may have similar issues if the same ethos is adopted.'

Meeting the assessment criteria

What not to include – don't include things that do not relate to the criteria that the Professional Registration and Accreditation Board are looking at. As an NVQ assessor, I got frustrated with the weight of irrelevant evidence that candidates submitted.

Key points for your Portfolio should be:

- address the criteria
- look for proof to demonstrate competency
- be ruthless in what you exclude
- pay attention to detail and presentation.

I ensured that in my application I demonstrated the attributes mentioned in the criteria and included evidence of my CPD activities over the past four to five years, together with conference papers and talks I had given at local, national and international conferences.

The assessment

Once I had completed my application and read it through very carefully (for spelling and grammar errors), I had done all I could and my fate was in the hands of the members of the Chartership Board (Professional Registration and Accreditation Board) who would assess my application. The Board has a total membership of 20. All are Chartered Members or Fellows. A number of those appointed have had experience of teaching at postgraduate level and/or of examining and assessing at all levels, including research degrees. The Board also appoints two external examiners to ensure that the Board complies with its regulations and procedures. With this information in mind, I was assured that my application would be treated professionally and fairly. I was pleased that my application would be assessed by my peers and other Fellows. It took me approximately three to four months to complete my submission. It seemed a long wait to hear from the Board. Finally, the assessment of my application was completed and it was positive – I was a Fellow!

The benefits of Fellowship

Fellowship has helped me with my career progression, enhancing my standing with other colleagues, and providing me with the personal satisfaction of achievement. One further advantage of receiving my Fellowship award is that the Open University Validation Service (OUVS) has agreed to award 75 Master's level credits for successful completion of Fellowship. The credit can be used in the OUVS Credit Accumulation and Transfer Scheme (CATS), and can be very beneficial to Chartered Fellows who may wish to pursue a higher degree, as it can be used towards obtaining qualifications in a number of disciplines, not just library and information studies, which is a temping offer and recognition of the high standard of this award within the academic environment and outside of the sector.

The application process genuinely helped me to reflect on and evaluate my achievements and lessons learned during my career so far and, perhaps more importantly, in assessing future opportunities and direction for my career path.

It was great if not a little nerve-racking to receive the award (the highest in the profession!) at Members' Day in front of friends, colleagues and peers all celebrating and recognizing achievement within the profession. I have my Fellowship certificate hanging on the wall in my office (adjacent to my Chartership certificate). I am immensely proud of it, and take pride in showing off this accolade to colleagues both within and outside the library sector.

If I can achieve Fellowship, so can you!

CASE STUDY 8.3
Pam Martindale: Using Twitter for professional registration

A lot of people dismiss Twitter as an inane social networking site where people tweet about what they had for breakfast and who is on *The X Factor*. It is true that some people do this but unlike the JISCMAIL lists you are not obliged to follow and receive ramblings and rants from people you are not interested in!

Used professionally, Twitter is an amazing resource and will alert you to news and events long before they hit the traditional sources of information. Following interesting people in your profession leads to increased knowledge (through following and reading the links they tweet to articles, blogs etc.), new relationships (if you respond to them and engage them in a discussion) and getting known outside your organization.

If you find it hard to travel to events and conferences it is really nice to be able to follow them in real time by following the conference hashtag (#); you can even comment on and interact with what is going on without leaving your office. The controversial 2013 CILIP AGM about rebranding was followed by far more people than those able to get to Birmingham and Umbrella 2013 was even trending nationally for a time. Collecting material in this way, adding your views and showing that you have built up a professional network is valuable evidence to demonstrate your wider professional awareness for both ACLIP and MCLIP. All discussions about Chartership, including the fortnightly Chartership chat, use the #Chartership hashtag, where you can ask questions and get support from peers, mentors and me!

I will admit I was sceptical at first but since I retired I have learned far more through Twitter than I ever did when I was working and have started to develop professional contacts around the country by tweeting about Chartership and other library related matters. It is nice, too, to attend a meeting with new colleagues and find you already 'know' them from their tweets.

As well as tweeting professionally, you should let your followers see a glimpse of your personality and the other things that interest you. Lots of librarians also tweet about their cats and knitting, sports they follow, books they read and places they travel to. Some people recommend that one in four tweets should be a retweet or a personal comment.

These are some useful Twitter accounts to follow to get started:

- @CILIPinfo, @CILIPSW, @CILIPcpd, @ARLGSW etc. (CILIP and its branches tweet news and events)
- @publibnews and @VftL_UK (info about what is happening in public libraries – if you work in an academic environment you need to know this stuff)
- @uklibchat (organizes monthly chats on a variety of useful topics like project management and leadership).

There are lots of books you can read telling you how to use Twitter and get the best from it, but mostly it is a matter of trial and error. The more you look at what people are saying the more you will discover new and interesting people to follow (look at who other people are following and talking to). Give it a go, you will not be disappointed. Just be warned, it can become addictive!!

Pam Martindale
Twitter@MartindalePam

9

The final steps

Gathering all your documentation and drafting your personal statement will take time but there will come a point where you have to decide that you are ready to submit. It is really important to set yourself a target date for submission, as it is very tempting just to continue compiling information and rewriting sections. Nothing sharpens the mind like a definite date for submitting. Your mentor may help you to do this by ensuring that you are being realistic and that you meet intermediate deadlines for your meeting or consultation with them.

At this stage you should go to the CILIP VLE, look at the level of professional registration for which you are working and click on the tab 'Assembling your Portfolio'. Here you will find all the information you need.

As you reach the final steps in building your Portfolio remember to consider four important questions:

- Have you got all the required elements of your Portfolio?
- Is the structure and layout of your Portfolio clear and is the Portfolio presented well for the assessors?
- Have you done a final check against the assessment criteria?
- Have you proofread your Portfolio or, preferably, got someone else to check it?

So much work will have gone into the various stages of building your Portfolio and it is crucial you don't slip up at this point.

Portfolio checklist

It seems such a simple thing to say, but you must go back to the handbook and check that you have assembled all the required elements of your Portfolio. If an element is missing or incorrectly submitted your Portfolio will be returned and that may cause quite a delay in the whole process of assessment. Each qualification has a checklist.

Certification

This is the Certification checklist:

- evaluative statement (maximum 1000 words)
- CV
- evidence to support your evaluative statement
- job description
- initial PKSB
- current PKSB
- mentor/mentee completion form.

Chartership

This is the Chartership checklist:

- evaluative statement (maximum 1000 words)
- CV
- evidence to support your evaluative statement
- job description
- initial PKSB
- current PKSB
- mentor/mentee completion form.

Fellowship

This is the Fellowship checklist:

- evaluative statement (maximum 1000 words)
- CV
- evidence to support your evaluative statement
- job description
- initial PKSB
- current PKSB
- letters of support from Chartered Members or senior colleagues, one of whom must be your mentor.

Revalidation

This is the Revalidation checklist:

- evaluative statement (maximum 250 words)
- CPD activity log.

Structure and presentation

You have all your required elements gathered – and now you have to decide how to organize your Portfolio using the CILIP Portfolio. The arrangement of your Portfolio is for you to decide, but whatever structure you decide on must enable the assessor to find all the relevant information easily.

Once you have organized your Portfolio and put the cross-references in your evaluative statement, you should make a final check that your Portfolio meets the assessment criteria. Re-read the assessment criteria and then read through the whole Portfolio. There is still time to revise or edit! But remember not to lose sight of your target date for submission.

The final step before submission is to share your Portfolio with your mentor or a critical friend. You can do this through the VLE. Your mentor will have seen most of the items previously so it should not take too long. If you are using a critical friend, who will have to be a registered Member of CILIP if you wish to share your Portfolio with them, and wish them to comment on the content as well as proofreading the text, ask them to look at the online handbook. Ask them to be honest. It is better to revise at this stage and avoid problems later down the line. I am sure you will have used a spell-check programme but do not rely on that for proofreading. I believe it is so much better anyway for another person to look at your completed Portfolio, if at all possible. Not only can they check spelling and grammar, they can also check for sense and completeness.

Now you are ready to submit your Portfolio, following the instructions in the VLE under the tab 'Submitting your application'.

What next?

Your Portfolio will be sent by the CILIP Professional Registration Team online to two assessors. They will use only the assessment criteria, with which you should now be very familiar, and will discuss their views. As a member of the Professional Registration and Accreditation Board I know how much work goes into the assessment. Assessors look at the whole Portfolio to determine whether you have met the criteria.

What happens if you hear that you have been asked to provide further information?

Don't panic. This means that you have failed to meet one of the criteria and you will be given very clear instructions about what is needed. Read those instructions carefully. Talk them through with your mentor or a critical friend.

If the initial assessors do not think that your Portfolio meets the assessment criteria, then it will go to a third assessor. If all three assessors agree that the Portfolio does not meet the assessment criteria, you will be informed that your application has been unsuccessful and given feedback as to why this is the case. You can resubmit when you feel ready to do so. You should discuss the feedback with your mentor or with a new mentor if you prefer.

If the three assessors do not agree, then your application will be discussed by the whole Professional Registration and Accreditation Board and a decision will be made based on a majority vote.

The feedback in either case will be a composite version of the views of all the assessors involved in the decision. It is important that you look carefully at this and use it as support for putting together your new Portfolio.

However, if you have followed the guidelines in the handbooks, the advice given in this book – especially the information from the various contributors – and all the information on CILIP's website, then hopefully the outcome should be successful. So then you celebrate!

I have spoken to many successful colleagues, whether they applied for Certification, Chartership, Fellowship or Revalidation, and we all share the pride in our success and our achievement. To belong to a professional association and to be judged by your peers as worthy of the CILIP award is a great feeling. Hopefully, the good habits you have got into as you compiled your Portfolio will continue and you will truly become a reflective practitioner.

Hints and tips

- Set a date for submission and plan your time to achieve that.
- Check you have all the required elements of your Portfolio.
- Prepare a draft contents page and make sure that the Portfolio is organized to help the assessors find all the information easily.
- Look at the assessment criteria again before you submit your Portfolio and double-check that you have included evidence for all assessment criteria.
- Check that your evidence is cross-referenced from your personal statement.
- Ask someone else to proofread your submission.
- Celebrate your success!

CASE STUDY 9.1
Linda Coombs: Chartership using the VLE

The new Chartership regulations have significantly changed the process of putting together a Portfolio, but the fundamental task of meeting the assessment criteria and highlighting reflection remain unchanged.

As virtual learning environments (VLEs) go, the CILIP one is simple to use. However, if you have little experience of VLEs, it can be daunting to construct a Portfolio on one. The video tutorials give a quick grounding in the basic functions of the platform, and are worth watching whether you are familiar with other VLEs or not. The tutorials cover uploading content to the VLE, sharing content with others, and submitting your Portfolio. Once you have started to upload content you may find that a structure needs to be imposed on the material. I did this by placing each reflection (which would have been my appendices in a printed version) on a new page, with evidence such as pictures as links from this page. You can provide navigational help for readers by including a link to the contents list and evaluative statement on every page. My Portfolio centred on the evaluative statement, which cross-referenced each reflection in the text, as well as having a full list at the side. No doubt as the VLE develops, and more people use it, more ideas for how to structure Portfolios will emerge.

It is easier to share

The new VLE makes sharing and reviewing the Portfolio significantly easier – mainly by having the Portfolio available online. For instance, once it is shared with your mentor, they are able to see the most recent version whenever they like, which was impossible under the old system. My mentor, Kate Marshall, said 'As a mentor I found it simple, convenient and very useful to be able to review mentee material online.' Having your Portfolio online makes it easier to fit in time to work on it, without the need for paper files or e-mail attachments. Finally, Portfolio submission has been simplified. This is now just a matter of a few clicks of the mouse, rather than the printing and mailing of duplicate copies – something that helped persuade me to use the new regulations.

Focus on the criteria

When writing content for the Portfolio focus on the criteria, after all this is what determines a pass or fail. When I considered submitting under the new regulations, I was put off by the fact that I had already written several reflections tailored to the old criteria. However, on closer inspection it is clear that the new criteria map easily onto the old. The new criteria are also more user friendly, with expansion and explanations given in the Chartership handbook. By far the most time consuming aspect was completing the PKSB. This is a comprehensive document covering the spectrum of skills and knowledge an information professional may use. It can highlight areas of strength and weakness, as well as topics which may not be relevant to your current role but could be avenues for development. The PKSB can arguably be the single most useful part of the Portfolio. At a qualifications (Professional Registration) workshop, I was advised to fill in the PKSB as a tool for personal reflection, rather than as a formal assessed piece of work. It is not necessary to complete the whole document in detail, as it inevitably covers areas that will not be relevant to you and your role.

Time to reflect

Regardless of how you end up using the VLE or PKSB, it is worth remembering that most people who do not pass Chartership do so because they have not been reflective enough. Personally, I found the reflection required to build the Portfolio more useful than any training I attended, simply because it gave me a chance to assess my own and my service performance and apply improvements directly. Others have found the process helped them to 'clarify medium and long term career goals'.

When bringing together my Portfolio I was aware of the importance of reflection and the value of the assessors' time. I tried to include only the supporting evidence which demonstrated my fulfilment of the criteria, using pictures as evidence where possible, and cutting out irrelevant parts of documents, as even though printing and sending the Portfolio no longer limits size, several people are giving up their time to read it.

Ultimately, while the new Chartership regulations have significantly changed the process of putting together a Portfolio, the fundamental task of meeting the assessment criteria and highlighting reflection remain unchanged. Therefore the new regulations only make this process of personal reflection and development easier and more convenient.

CASE STUDY 9.2
Chloe French: The Chartership experience

Compiling a Portfolio of professional development is a daunting challenge and at the start of the process, like many other Chartership candidates, I felt overwhelmed by the task that lay ahead of me. I embarked on the Chartership process within a year of completing my library and information studies Master's qualification. I knew the process would be very different from the academic one to which I was accustomed, but that I would need to apply the same methodical approach in order to create a successful Portfolio.

One of the most important things I learned is that it takes time to develop a full understanding of the Chartership process and how to create an effective Portfolio. My first step was to gather information about Portfolio building, as this was an entirely new form of assessment for me. I read the Chartered Membership handbook and articles from CILIP's list of suggested reading. I collected features offering Portfolio advice from the *Library and Information Gazette* (now *CILIP Update*) and from *Impact*, the journal of CILIP's Career Development Group. I attended a Chartership advisory course where I met fellow Chartership candidates. There is a lot of information to absorb in the initial stages, but with time it all starts to make sense.

This was the first time I had written a development plan, but with the help of an experienced mentor I was introduced to the concept of self-directed learning. I learned valuable strategies for identifying and expressing my training and development needs. My Chartership journey became much clearer once I had identified these needs, established how I would meet them and what I would learn on the way. At this stage I decided that the aim of my Portfolio would be to demonstrate my development in the early stages of my professional career.

Gathering the evidence

With these clear goals established I then focused on undertaking the training identified in my development plan and gaining experience in my everyday job. Initially I gathered pieces of evidence demonstrating my development from all areas of my work. There was no form of selection at this stage. I wanted to collect as much as I could, so that I would be able to choose the most suitable examples to enter into the final Portfolio. For example, I kept a log of training events I attended, certificates of attendance, meeting agendas and minutes, as well as examples of my everyday work. Yet I still felt uneasy about how I would present this evidence in my Portfolio. Again, it took time for me to work out the best ways to present all the information I had gathered.

I reviewed my ever-increasing collection of evidence at regular intervals – often in preparation for a meeting with my mentor. These meetings provided the opportunity to reflect on the progress I was making. Each time we met, my understanding of the Chartership process improved, as did my confidence in my Portfolio-building skills.

Preparing the Portfolio

About ten months into the Chartership process I began to contemplate how I would build my Portfolio. At this point I decided to consult a couple of examples of successful submissions to see different ways of organizing all the necessary documentation. I found this both encouraging and a little unsettling, because they were very different from what I was preparing, but it was important to remember that a Portfolio is a very personal document and that each candidate will approach the task in their own distinctive way.

Once I had completed the actions in my development plan it was time to commit to compiling the Portfolio. I set about this in the way I had always done with academic exercises, simply because I knew this worked for me. I re-read all the information supplied by CILIP to ensure I understood the assessment criteria and then I wrote out the criteria and stuck them on the wall in front of my desk. This would ensure that everything I included in the Portfolio related to the assessment criteria and that I was always writing reflectively – analysing my performance and considering the impact of training events on my professional development.

I chose to divide my evaluative statement, and consequently the pieces of evidence, into sections based on the assessment criteria. In the first section I introduced myself and presented my development plan. In the second I analysed my personal performance, focusing on the core areas of my professional development. In the third, I evaluated the performance of the library service for which I work. In the final section I displayed my commitment to CPD by reflecting on developmental events I had attended and by providing details of my professional reading and the ways I had used this within my job.

Writing the evaluative statement requires discipline in order to present the relevant information within the word limit. I chose to offer brief initial analysis in the personal statement with an immediate reference to the relevant piece of evidence in the appendices section. The evidence section of the Portfolio was my opportunity to elaborate on my professional development. My aim was to present a clear picture to an assessor who might have very little knowledge of my sector. As well as remembering to address the relevant assessment criteria, I also knew that I had to make the report easy and inviting to read. Consequently, I wanted to present my evidence in a variety of formats. For example, I chose to present some training events in a table so that it was clear to see at a glance the courses I had attended, what I had learned and how I would apply this new knowledge to my job. For other courses I included a certificate of attendance and a piece of reflective writing highlighting what I had gained from the experience.

Conclusion

Compiling a Portfolio of professional development marked my transition from an academic to a professional style of writing and presenting information. I used the writing and analytical skills I had developed at university, but this time I was applying them to myself. Building my Portfolio has equipped me with the skills to analyse my strengths and weaknesses and take control of my learning and development. I have become more self-aware and have developed the habit of not just acquiring new skills, but reflecting on how these improve my ability to perform my job. Taking responsibility for your learning and development is a challenge, but also an essential workplace skill. Chartership and creating a Portfolio were demanding tasks, but critically analysing your performance is rarely easy. The time and effort I put into the creation of my Portfolio resulted in a document of which I am proud and, more importantly, has developed in me a set of skills which will prove invaluable throughout my career.

CASE STUDY 9.3
Shamin Renwick: The Fellowship experience

> The difference between a job and a career is the difference between forty and sixty hours a week.
>
> Robert Frost

Thanks to the ubiquitous nature of information technology today, those hours could be increased and need not be restricted to a desk at the office. My appreciation and commitment to the profession has been my driving force as I truly enjoy being a librarian.

Having had the pleasure and opportunity to serve at the executive level of our national association as well as at the highest level in the regional library association (as President of the Association of Caribbean University, Research and Institutional Libraries [ACURIL] in 2003–4), I wanted to be involved in the profession at an international level. Coming from a developing society, getting involved in CILIP in the UK, as well as others, such as the American Library Association (ALA) and IFLA, would be a natural expansion to gain experience and keep up to date with professional activities at an advanced level, which should in turn impact on my work in the region.

Dr Alma Jordan MCLIP, former University Librarian at University of the West Indies and a long-standing Member of The Library Association, was instrumental in my getting involved in CILIP. In keeping abreast of CILIP's activities through its comprehensive and well structured website, I noted the criteria for becoming a Fellow and felt that if my application was successful, there would only be positive outcomes.

Being unable to access any of the substantial preparation, training and mentorship provided to Members living in the UK, I decided to adhere closely to the application guidelines, which I studied in detail (translate: read, re-read and summarized). Little else about the process was available on the internet. I must say 'thanks' to the members of the Professional Development Department for managing the process efficiently.

The practice of maintaining a detailed CV over the years proved worthwhile, as this comprehensive record served me well when recalling activities and achievements I accomplished early in my career.

Several prominent librarians (local and regional) with whom I had collaborated over the years enthusiastically provided letters of support. Though great achievers themselves, only one was a Fellow of CILIP (FCLIP), so I explained the application procedures and the criteria to be satisfied.

Writing a personal statement was indeed quite a challenge, as it would be for all persons applying for Fellowship. It was written in three parts, matching the three areas in which a Fellow had to have substantial achievement: professional practice, contribution to all or part of the profession, and active commitment to professional development. I am grateful for comments and advice from Professor Derek Law, whom I asked to review my application.

An extremely useful task was preparing a carefully formatted document in which I rewrote my personal statement and inserted the relevant items of evidence for each point made. Typical of the stereotypical librarian who keeps everything, I had actually retained some documents (in pre-electronic typeface) over the years, unsure of whether they would ever be useful except for some nostalgic reason. They took me back to a time and place in my career where the possibility of acquiring the most prestigious qualification in the profession would not have occurred to me.

Gathering and presenting evidence

Gathering and selecting evidence, like my personal statement, required a great deal of thought and planning. Items of evidence could take different formats. The result of the work of committees, not just a list of committees, would be more meaningful. Letters from notable persons can support a perspective on an accomplishment; for example, a letter of commendation or congratulations for receiving an award instead of just a list of achievements can be submitted. Evidence could be an item at different periods of time; for example, an annual report written early in your career and one many years later could illustrate growth, both in ability to communicate as well as in duties undertaken and how you executed them as your career grew. Depending on the activity or point being presented, e-mail threads can provide an excellent record.

I paid a great deal of attention to the presentation of the entire Portfolio, ensuring that the formatting and organization made it uncomplicated to review. For easy reference, I gave each item of evidence a cover page with a statement of what it was, why I selected it, and a numbering system which linked it to the list of evidence. Double-checking for errors was essential, as this submission was a reflection of me and I would be judged on both content and presentation.

Reflections on achieving Fellowship

Some of the benefits of being elected to the register of Fellows are universal. Undoubtedly it brings tremendous prestige to one's name and reputation and, by association, to one's employer and other affiliations. Post-nominal letters are impressive and give professional authority to one's name. No one can deny the value in the world of academia where post-nominals, placed on business cards and next to signatures, are the standard by which achievements are recognized and celebrated, carrying a weight of authority and expertise. And in the case of the FCLIP, which is by no means a commonplace qualification even in the UK, this honour is greatly valued.

Recognition of one's achievements and commitment by the wider society, as sought through Fellowship, is welcome and necessary. It is a great motivation for the person being acknowledged to continue striving to perform at an even higher level, and underlines that service is not in vain. Like other small associations around the world, many national library associations in the Caribbean suffer from a lack of critical mass of members to make them work efficiently. The membership of the regional ACURIL is separated by water, distance, language and culture. Flagging attendance and lack of support for activities are endemic. It is my fervent hope that this achievement of the highest professional qualification can be seen as a reward and a much needed incentive to inspire colleagues who are similarly committed to the profession, continuing education and volunteer service, as they seek the betterment of themselves and their organizations.

Acknowledgement is necessary and Fellowship is one way to gain this. I hope that Fellowship can be seen as a tangible goal to work towards for colleagues who may no longer be striving for academic achievement but wish to contribute to professional practice in a meaningful way.

The opportunity for self-reflection was greatly valued. The thought process involved in self-appraisal, which probably would not be undertaken under other circumstances, was most beneficial and appreciated. No other task undertaken over the years called for this degree of introspection and self-evaluation. Having to analyse, admit to oneself, document and justify to others one's thoughts about oneself was a revealing exercise.

Over the years, we work dedicatedly, often moving from project to project, occasionally wondering why, and sometimes feeling unappreciated. My career has taken several unexpected turns, challenges have been many and, as experienced by us all at some time or other, there has been unavoidable professional jealousy; factors which can deter one from working towards laudable goals. So attaining Fellowship status has provided a much needed justification for my career, especially when time is taken from family, as vacations are all working ones and stress levels are generally high. It has engendered in me a sense of overcoming obstacles and that maintaining my planned course was worthwhile.

The honour bestowed by being granted the highest professional qualification from an esteemed institution like CILIP gave me a sense of personal fulfilment unrivalled by other achievements to date. It was a major highlight in my career so far and, I am sure, will number among the most valued at the end of it.

The experience of preparing the Portfolio has enhanced my skills in self-assessment, assessing others and acquiring managerial skills important in human resource tasks, such as the selection and recruitment of staff. It provided processes and procedures which I can use for other projects requiring analysis and documentation. It has enhanced my standing in the profession, recognizing my seniority, and provides authority for my position as a mentor.

Having to reflect on and analyse the path of my career, taking note of changes in direction and why I had made the choices I did, how much I had achieved and where my support came from, was invaluable in taking stock of my entire life thus far. It has prepared me to go on to another level of existence – a new phase of my career and life, opening up a whole new world.

CASE STUDY 9.4
Pooja Tejura: The Certification experience

Using the VLE

In the first instance I actually completed a paper draft for submission under the old criteria, which I was not in time to submit. Therefore, when the new criteria were announced, I had to get to grips with the idea of submitting electronically through the VLE. I understand that VLEs are fairly common in HE institutes but it took some time for me to get to grips with the VLE and work out how to structure my Portfolio page. The screencasts were useful and without them I would not have been able to set up my Portfolio page and submit my project.

Professional and Knowledge Skills Base

The Professional and Knowledge Skills Base (PKSB) is a wonderful tool to help a library and information professional to assess their development independently and it was introduced as the main change under the new criteria. Without the PKSB I could not have objectively reviewed my time as a library assistant. However, the PKSB is also a very daunting document to get to grips with. It is long, complex and contains many abstract terms and concepts to entry level library professionals. It takes time to be able to use it effectively.

I think we need to encourage organizations to adopt it more widely as a developmental plan for all employees.

Understanding the criteria

The assessment criteria are quite difficult to understand and I felt a need for more online evidence as well as guidance from my mentor.

Reflective writing

I found reflective writing a useful process and I believe it strengthened my Portfolio. Many of the pieces I wrote were guided by my CILIP mentor who asked me to continually reflect on what I was learning or what difference my activity or event was making to the organization. As part of this process I felt I needed to reflect on Sutton Library Service as an organization, its constituent branch libraries and my role as a library assistant. I knew I was ready to submit when I realized that after considering my current experience and role there was not much else for me to reflect on!

Working with a mentor

Working with a mentor was a new process for me. For my Master's degree I worked with my supervisor but I found the mentor and mentee process as part of CILIP Certification far more intense and important to achieving a successful outcome, especially as the criteria are new.

I relied heavily on my mentor's experience and we exchanged several e-mails as she reviewed successive drafts of my documents. The mentor–mentee relationship is a very important part of the learning and submission process.

Building my Portfolio

I kept application to CILIP confidential for personal reasons but I know that gathering evidence from work should not be as difficult as I found it. Evidence in any form should be sufficient, provided it corroborates the activity or event. The emphasis is on the reflective writing process which follows the activity under discussion.

The evaluative statement

The evaluative statement is only 1000 words. It is very tight and therefore every word should count. Candidates need to understand what the permitted deductions are so that they can correctly calculate their word count.

Portfolio checklist

There is a Portfolio checklist of documents on the VLE, which tells you that you are ready to submit. However, my actual list is longer than that online list. I included a list of abbreviations, bibliography, table of contents, mentoring log and mentoring agreement. Inclusion of these documents is more in line with the old Certification criteria than the new criteria but I included them anyway on the advice of my mentor.

Submission

It is essential to follow the steps for submission carefully to find out how to pay, be reminded that the project cannot be changed once submitted, learn how to give access to relevant assessors, and a have a look at the final Portfolio checklist.

Bibliography and references

Booth, A. and Brice, A. (eds) (2004) *Evidence-based Practice for Information Professionals: a handbook*, Facet Publishing.

Boud, D., Keogh, R. and Walker, D. (1985) *Reflection: turning experience into learning*, Kogan Page.

Boydell, T. and Leary, M. (1986) *Identifying Training Needs*, Institute of Personnel and Development.

Brine, A. (2005) *Continuing Professional Development: a guide for information professionals*, Chandos.

Brine, A. and Feather, J. (2003) Building a Skills Portfolio for the Information Professional, *New Library World*, 104 (1194/1195), 455–63.

Cameron, J. (1997) *The Vein of Gold: a journey to your creative heart*, Pan.

Chapman, J. (1991) *Journaling for Joy: writing your way to personal growth and freedom*, Newcastle Publishing.

Dakers, H. (1996) *NVQs and How to Get Them*, Kogan Page.

Gibbs, G. (1988) *Learning by Doing: a guide to teaching and learning methods*, Further Educational Unit, Oxford Polytechnic.

Hall, F. and Barker, C. (2005) Producing a Portfolio, *Impact*, **8** (4), 81–2.

Honey, P. and Mumford, A. (1986) *The Manual of Learning Styles*, Peter Honey.

Honey, P. and Mumford, A. (2000) *The Learning Styles Helper's Guide*, Peter Honey.

Hood, I. (2006) Practical Portfolio Tips, *Library and Information Gazette*, 2 June.

Jackson, N. (2001) *Personal Development Planning: what does it mean?* PDP Working Paper 1, Learning and Teaching Subject Network Generic Centre.

Kay, D. and Hinds, R. (2009) *A Practical Guide to Mentoring*, 4th edn, How to Books.

Klauser, H. A. (1986) *Writing on Both Sides of the Brain: breakthrough techniques for people who write*, Harper & Row.

Kolb, D. (1986) *Experiential Learning: experience as the source of learning and development*, Prentice Hall.

Marshall, K. (2006) The Chartership Process and Planning for Continuing Professional Development, *Impact*, **9** (1), 4–5.

McKee, B. (2006) Sustaining CILIP: some questions answered, *Library & Information Update*, April, 5 (4), 20–1.

Raddon, R. (ed.) (2005) *Your Career, Your Life: career management for the information professional*, Ashgate.

Rolfe, G., Freshwater, D. and Jasper, M. (2001) *Critical Reflection for Nursing and the Helping Professions: a user's guide*, Palgrave.

Schön, D. (1983) *The Reflective Practitioner: how professionals think in action*, Basic Books.

Thomson, B. (2006) *Growing People: learning and developing from day to day experience*, Chandos.

Watts, A. W. (1957) *The Way of Zen*, Penguin.

Webb, S. and Grimwood-Jones, D. (2003) *Personal Development in the Information and Library Profession*, 3rd edn, Europa.

Williamson, M. (1986) *Training Needs Analysis*, Library Association Publishing.

Websites

Andrew Gibbons, www.andrewgibbons.co.uk.

CILIP: Professional Knowledge and Skills Base, www.cilip.org.uk/pksb.

CILIP Professional Registration,

www.cilip.org.uk/cilip/jobs-and-careers/qualifications-and-professional-development/cilip-qualifications.

CILIP Virtual Learning Environment, http://vle.cilip.org.uk.

Index